# SACRED ENERGIES OF THE SUN & MOON

"Once again, Erika Buenaflor has provided us with a marvelous understanding of the ancient shamanic mysteries of Mesoamerica. All ancient pre-Columbian civilizations utilized the movements of the sun, moon, and stars to understand their earthly existence. *Sacred Energies of the Sun and Moon* allows us to glimpse behind the veil of the mundane to view the esoteric synchronization of the heavens as they influence our health and everyday life."

Antonio "Dr. Tony" Zavaleta, Ph.D.,
coauthor of *Curandero Conversations*

"Erika is the real deal. As a millennial Latina looking to reconnect with my spiritual roots, she has been a go-to resource for me and many others like me. She's very knowledgeable about the various types of spiritual modalities, and the time and dedication she devotes to learning and researching these ancient practices is a feat unto itself. Anyone looking to learn more about traditional and indigenous spirituality should read Erika's books."

Mariela Rosario,
editor in chief of HipLatina

"In *Sacred Energies of the Sun and Moon,* Erika Buenaflor does a superb job of blending a well-documented history of Mesoamerican curanderismo and shamanic beliefs while also providing a practical guide for modern souls to bring the energy of the sun and moon into their daily life."

Kara Dellacioppa, Ph.D., director of the Faculty Development Center at California State University, Dominguez Hills

"Now more than ever we look to the sun and the moon to guide us through unprecedented times. I am grateful for the gift of this book, allowing us to connect to our ancient Mesoamerican indigenous traditions to provide healing and wisdom at a time when it is greatly needed."

Rocio Rosales Meza, Ph.D., intuitive healer and energy worker

# SACRED ENERGIES OF THE SUN & MOON

*Shamanic Rites of Curanderismo*

ERIKA BUENAFLOR, M.A., J.D.

Bear & Company
Rochester, Vermont

Bear & Company
One Park Street
Rochester, Vermont 05767
www.BearandCompanyBooks.com

Text stock is SFI certified

Bear & Company is a division of Inner Traditions International.



Cataloging-in-Publication Data for this title is available from the Library of Congress.

ISBN 978-1-59143-378-1 (print)
ISBN 978-1-59143-379-8 (ebook)

Printed and bound in the United States by Lake Book Manufacturing, Inc.
The text stock is SFI certified. The Sustainable Forestry Initiative® program promotes sustainable forest management.

10 9 8 7 6 5 4 3

Text design and layout by Virginia Scott Bowman
This book was typeset in Garamond Premier Pro, Gill Sans, and Futura with Le Havre and NixRift used as display typefaces.

To send correspondence to the author of this book, mail a first-class letter to the author c/o Inner Traditions • Bear & Company, One Park Street, Rochester, VT 05767, and we will forward the communication, or contact the author directly at **www.realizeyourbliss.com**.

*Dedicated to my sun and moon,*
*my husband, Miguel Buenaflor*

# Contents

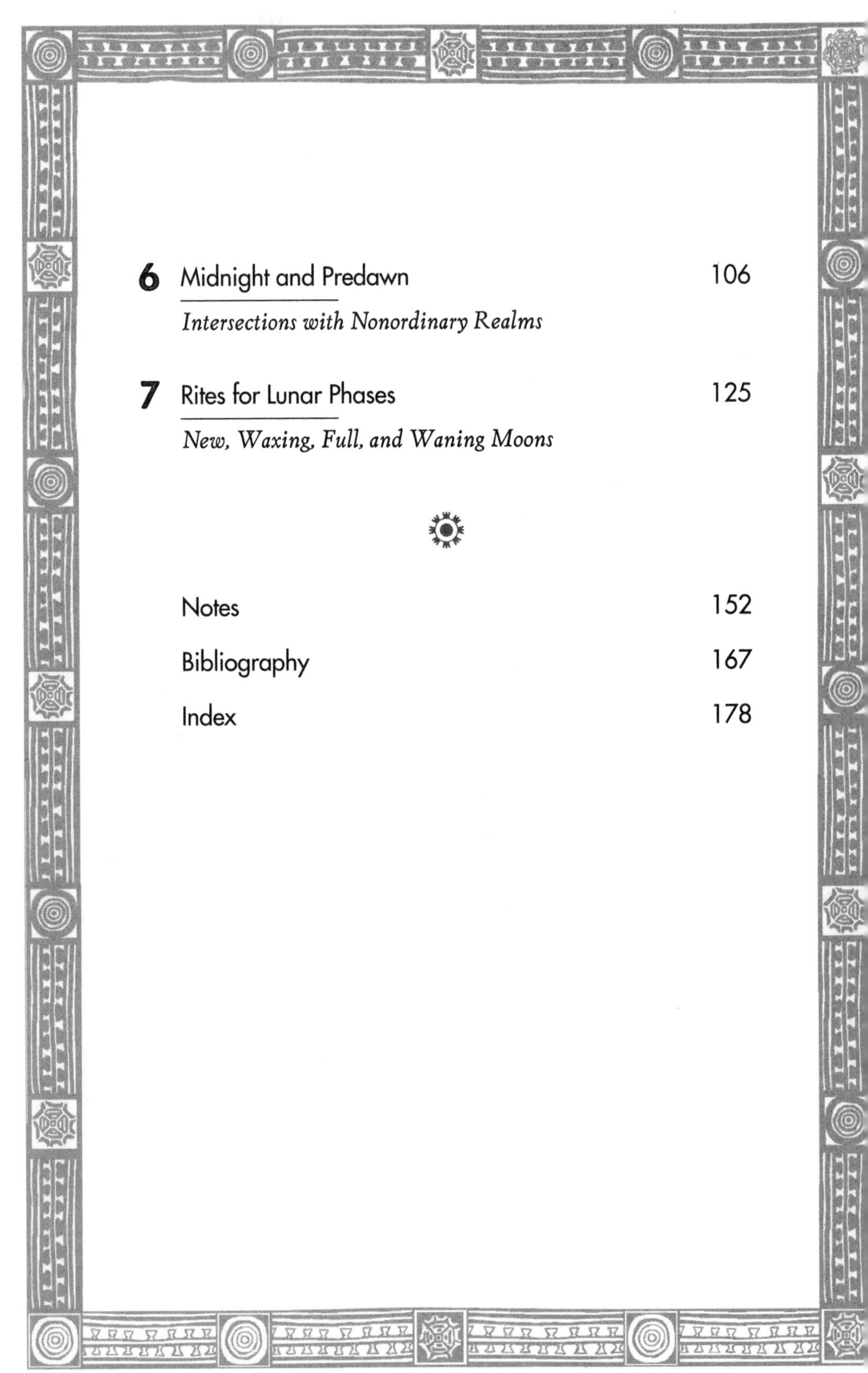

# Introduction to Ancient Mesoamerican Shamanic Solar and Lunar Rites

Ancient Mesoamerican peoples lived in unison with nature and its daily cycles. They used this sacred wisdom to empower their shamanic rites and intentions, knowing that certain times of the day and night exude particular energies that are more advantageous for different rites. Sacred rites of invocation, healing, cleansing, birthing, rebirthing, purification, rejuvenation, and manifestation were performed by most of the people, not just by shamans. Because they believed the sun to be the principal source of soul or sacred essence energy, they carried out rites at specific times of the day to utilize this energy to its maximum potential.

These solar and lunar rites instill self-awareness, self-love, and self-empowerment.

In this book, I will outline how we can use this ancient indigenous wisdom for healing and to be more mindful, live in the present, manifest with greater impeccability, and approach life as a sacred practice. By utilizing the rhythms of daily and nightly cycles, we can become more in tune with ourselves. We can know more clearly what makes us happy and what we need to do to bring it to fruition.

Rituals that tap into the natural energies and magic of the sun, night sun, and moon can align us toward more harmonious states of being. We know ideal times to heal, recharge, release, perform *limpias* (shamanic cleanses that holistically purify spaces and individuals), manifest certain intentions, attract ideal synchronicities, and much more.

The ideas and values undergirding these rites are influenced both by ancient indigenous practices and by the teachings of my curanderx* mentors. Curanderx are the practitioners of curanderismo. Although this dynamic Latin American shamanic practice incorporates Judeo-Christian (especially Catholic), Native American, Caribbean, Spanish, Moorish, and African practices and beliefs, its roots lie in the beliefs, practices, and methodologies of the indigenous peoples of the Americas. I did most of my training as a curandera in the Yucatán with two curanderx who had lived all of their lives in the Yucatán, and with two others who were trained in Yucatec Maya practices and were also versed in Mexica or Nahua† shamanic traditions. My practices have also been influenced by more than two decades of training and experience as a curandera, and by my interests in self-directed neuroplasticity—the brain's ability to change structurally and functionally through repetition.

To illuminate the ideas underlying these solar and lunar rites, I will draw from their mythologies; architectural designs and layouts, which simulate solar and lunar hierophanies (manifestations of the sacred);[1] sixteenth- and seventeenth-century enthnohistorical records; precontact and postcontact codices;‡ and precontact art-

*I have decided to follow the trend of progressive Latinx communities, who are using *x* in the place of *as/os* at the end of gendered words to transcend static gender binaries. *Curanderx* is pronounced *curanderex.*

†The terms *Mexica* and *Nahua* have often been used interchangeably to talk about the same group of people in the Aztec empire. Since I am principally focusing on the dominant Mexica tribe of the Aztec empire in this book, I use the term *Mexica* rather than *Aztec* or *Nahua*. I use *Aztec empire* to describe the many different indigenous peoples living on the Anahuac plateau at the time of the Spaniards' arrival in 1519.

‡I use the term *precontact* to denote the period prior to the arrival of the Spaniards in 1519 and *postcontact* for the period after their arrival.

work. Mesoamerican anthropologist Traci Ardren asserts, "Memory as a layer of identity is accessible to archaeologists through tangible monuments and the practices or performances that accompanied such charged places."[2] Rituals and their performances are languages that generate meanings in the specific context of other sets of meaningful actions and discourses.[3]

I will also describe the performances and instruments of these rituals, because these were all critical elements for the rituals' success. More specifically, I will consider the identities of the actors—the shamans and recipients—as well as the costuming, accessories, and sacred tools that were used; the portrayals and embodiments of deities; and the performances, body postures, and timing of these rituals.

I will use these sources to infer what these people knew about the energies of the solar and lunar periods, how they utilized such knowledge to ensure the success of specific intentions, and how we can use such wisdom to help us live healthier and happier lives. At the very least, these rites can arouse positive emotions, enhancing physical, emotional, mental, and spiritual well-being. Ideally, we can also invite more synchronistic magic in our lives and learn how to consciously work with the energies and cycles of the sun and moon.

## RITUAL PERFORMANCES AND ACTORS

Ritual performances and symbolic instruments serve as modes of communication and social action. They give meaning to existence by providing a model of the world, both as it is and as it ought to be. They also impart a set of ultimate values that reflect the beliefs and attitudes underlying rituals.[4] Theoretician Catherine Bell notes that rituals do not simply express sentiments of collective harmony; they also channel conflict, focus grievances, socialize participants, negotiate power relations, and, ultimately, forge images by which participants can think of themselves as an embracing unity. Of course these effects depend on many factors, such as the degree of people's involvement in the rites, the amount of repetition, and the degree to which the values embodied in the ritual are reinforced in other areas of social life.[5]

Deities associated with the sun or moon were typically invoked, honored, embodied, or portrayed and could come forth and partake in these ceremonies in diverse ways. These deities could manifest in a quadripartite form, corresponding to the four world directions; in a dual form, reflecting oppositions between various realms of the cosmos or opposite periods of the day; or in a single form. They could combine aspects of many levels of existence, with or without zoomorphic characteristics.[6]

The gender, age, and class of the performers were critical to the success of these rites, as each category lent itself to the invocation, embodiment, or portrayal of the deities in different ways. Certain genders were associated with certain traits and abilities. The generative and regenerative nature of the Earth was typically associated with the feminine.[7] The masculine was often associated with strength, virility, and potency. Third-gender deities could combine many levels of existence and were generally identified with transformation, particularly during seasonal transitions, which were understood as periods of liminality and flux.[8]

In examining these ancient rites, I approach gender in a manner like that of many anthropologist feminist theoreticians, including Joan Gero, Elizabeth Brumfiel, and Judith Butler. I differentiate sex—the physiological differences between males and females—from gender, a socially constructed category. Gender is not an immutable entity determined simply by biophysiological features, nor is it a static set of relationships or characteristics. Rather, gender is a social construction that is continuously negotiated, reconstituted, and performed in diverse manners.[9] I examine the manner in which gender was constructed and conveyed in these performances.

I use the concept *third-gender* not to indicate an instantiated "blurred" sex, but as a way to communicate a space of infinite gendered possibilities.[10] Within this category I include the notions of dual-gendered, two-spirited, mixed-gender, ambiguously gendered, and androgynous. I do not, however, include the concepts of gender crossing or hermaphrodism in the term *third-gender*. Gender crossing in the ancient Maya context has been identified as one sex attempting to impersonate the other sex.[11] For the Mexica, completely intersexed adult *potlaches* (hermaphrodites) were identified as women who possessed pronounced male biological traits and sexual habits.[12]

For the ancient Mesoamericans, the same costumes, personal ornaments, and sacred tools that conveyed femaleness or maleness could also be used to invoke, honor, and portray third-gender deities. For the Yucatec Maya, for example, a hip cloth or loincloth, sometimes coupled with a short skirt, generally signified maleness, while a skirt worn below the knee, sometimes accompanied by a long tunic-like *huipil,* related to femininity.[12] The ruler of Copán, Waxaklahun Ub'ah K'awil, commonly referred to as 18 Rabbit, as portrayed on Stela H at the central plaza of Classic-period Copán, wears a netted skirt typical of the male maize deity below the knee, coupled with a tunic like that of a woman. These features indicate that he is able to embody a third-gender deity.[14] Friar Bernardino de Sahagún, a sixteenth-century missionary and ethnographer, notes that a small *tlazoltectli* (broom) was placed in a baby girl's hand during the bathing rite, while a baby boy was given a shield.[15] The ritual instruments that shamans utilized to invoke Toci—grandmother of the Earth mother deity complex—included the shield, broom, weaving spindle and batten, and bathhouse.[16]

The age of the participants was also a crucial factor in ensuring the success of these rites. Different periods in life were associated with certain attributes, skills, and knowledge. Youth was generally associated with ripeness and proximity to the nonordinary realms—Upperworld, Middleworld, and Underworld—where supernatural beings dwelled.[17] Youth was also associated with the new moon and new moon rites. In ceremonial settings, old (postmenopausal) women and old men were portrayed when the moon or sun was seen as decreasing in strength and power.

Ancient Mesoamerica was stratified into classes, generally a noble class and a class of commoners. Among the Postclassic Mexica and Yucatec Maya, the highest political and religious posts were allotted to the noble classes. For instance, only nobles could become the high priests of the cults of Tlaloc, the rain god, and Huitzilopochtli, the tutelary war god.[18] The nobles had the privilege of attending the schools of higher education, where they learned rhetoric, divine hymns, divine speeches, the calendrical systems and their methods of divination and prophecies, the art of reading and writing, the administration of their sacraments, and the wisdom, traditions, and histories recorded in the codices. Particularly gifted commoners, however, were allowed to attend these schools.[19]

Although only nobles could lead certain ceremonies, most of the solar and lunar rites discussed in this book were practiced by all people, irrespective of class and gender. Sixteenth-century ethnographers Sahagún and Diego Durán both note the involvement of common people in these ceremonies as active agents. The spells and rituals documented by seventeenth-century ethnographer and missionary Hernando Ruiz de Alarcón demonstrate that common people, including farmers, hunters, fisherman, lime burners, and traveling merchants often used spells and rituals in their everyday practices. More abstruse matters, including soul retrieval, divination, and less common illnesses, were in the hands of shamanic specialists.[20] All the rites discussed in this book can be performed by lay people as well as shamans.

## SACRED INSTRUMENTS AND SETTINGS

Ritual instruments, settings, and symbols are inherently polysemic: they refer simultaneously to many levels of human experience and are susceptible to many meanings and interpretations. Ritual elements must be interpreted in terms of the positions they can occupy and in relation to the symbolic systems they generate.[21] In the codices, the sun and night sky, for example, can function as symbols separate from their roles as scenic indicators. The sun disk signifies the daylight hours and perhaps lightness in general, while the moon in a semicircle of night sky symbolizes generalized night or darkness. At other times, such as in the marriage almanacs, these symbols appear to signify a couple's prospects for having children.[22] The sun is used to depict the couples who are likely to have the most children; the moon and mixed moon and sun symbols denote couples who are likely to have fewer.[23]

The sacred objects and settings of these rites were understood as being alive: they had their own sacred essence energy (or soul energy) and agency. Ceremonies were performed to animate, sustain, and even terminate most of the material objects and settings—natural spaces, plazas, homes, temples, political spaces, and sweat baths.[24] Jade—whether worn by a noble in an elaborate beaded skirt or worn in artificial form by commoners who painted stones blue-green to imitate the real thing—"had an inherent agency to connect the wearer with the fertile power of the Maize Deity and a related set of regenerative forces."[25] The sacred settings of these ceremonies had agency as well. They facilitated a sacred space wherein the ritual actors could garner, emit, connect with, or embody the sacred nature and gifts of the sun, moon, or night sun.

## GOALS OF THIS BOOK

The principal aims of this book are twofold. First, I intend to inspire readers to move in rhythm and work with the sun, moon, and night sun in order to live happier and healthier lives, perform holistic healings and cleansings, manifest with greater impeccability, and revitalize the mind, body, spirit, and soul. The suggested mantras and ways to integrate ceremony in everyday life are meant for people with busy lifestyles who nevertheless want to treat life as a sacred ceremonial practice. Blurring the distinction between the sacred and profane often tends to instill gratitude, which is beneficial for overall well-being and increases favorable synchronicities. More elaborate ceremonies are provided for those who enjoy these rites and can invest further time and effort in them.

The second goal of this book is to decolonize and reclaim indigenous practices, traditions, and beliefs. As in my first book, *Cleansing Rites of*

*Curanderismo,* I would like to enact the healing power of epistemology—claiming these practices, traditions, and beliefs as worthy of further examination. I will critically examine different sources for these rites and place them in dialogue with each other so that we may deepen and possibly correct our understanding of them. Using this sacred wisdom can breathe magic, joy, and happiness into our lives.

In addition, I also hope to dispel any belief that human sacrifice was the predominant ceremonial activity of Mesoamerican peoples. For both the Maya and the Aztec empire, human sacrifice was typically a state-sponsored event. The majority of Mesoamerican peoples did not perform human sacrifice.[26] Objects found at sites where common people resided were those used for curing and divination, incense burners, figurines, long-handled censers, and musical instruments.[27]

## BREAKDOWN OF BOOK

The first two chapters of this book will set the stage for the ancient Mexica's and Maya's ardent focus on and love for the sun, night sun, and moon. The first chapter will explain their principally four-part division of a day, their creation mythologies concerning the sun and moon, their architectural hierophanies of the sun and moon, and the emulations of the sun and moon by nobles and rulers. The second chapter will introduce the dynamic and fluid nature of their solar- and lunar-related deities, who were often honored during their solar and lunar rites.

Chapters three through seven examine the ancient solar and lunar rites of the ancient Mexica and Maya and how we can utilize this sacred wisdom to live happier and healthier lives. Each of these chapters is broken down into three sections: (1) a discussion of the ancient Mexica and Maya solar and lunar rites, (2) practical rites, rituals, and mantras we can incorporate into our everyday lives to utilize these sacred energies, and (3) finally, more elaborate rites for those who are able, ready, and willing to invest more time. Before discussing the recommended rites, I also include a list of associated sacred items, activities, and deities (describing their garb, instruments, and body paint) for those who would like to create more elaborate rites or incorporate these ancient indigenous traditions into their own ceremonies.

## BENEFITS OF SOLAR AND LUNAR RITES

Being mindful and present, preferably in a state of gratitude, when engaging in these rites will yield benefits for the mind, body, spirit, and soul. The ceremonies promote positive mental and emotional states and healthy lifestyles. They also establish a stronger connection with the divine as expressed in nature and with its magic and gifts.

On a practical level, repeated use of rites can result in greater neuroplasticity, changing neural pathways, creating denser synapses in the brain, and triggering the birth of new neurons.[28] The rites incorporate visualization of enjoyable images, positive affirming mantras, meditative activities, and activities that promote mindfulness, all of which have been proved to result in self-directed neuroplasticity.[29]

Repeated engagement in activities of this kind can manage depression (without medication), reduce stress, and eliminate mind chatter and its associated emotions. It can also reverse age-related brain atrophy, decrease anxiety, develop emotional intelligence and compassion, and reduce high blood pressure.[30] Cognitive functions can see improvement after as little as twenty minutes a day for four repeated days.[31] Of course, the extent and permanence of these benefits will increase the more we engage in these activities regularly and mindfully.

Many of these rites also stimulate meditative or trance states characterized by alpha and theta* brain rhythms, which help self-directed neuroplasticity take effect.[32]

---

*Alpha brain waves (8–12 Hz) are typically experienced when daydreaming, in a relaxed state, or right before falling asleep. Theta brain waves (4–7 Hz) are usually present in deep meditation or in a light sleep, including the REM (rapid eye movement) dream state. Theta is often identified as the state in which we experience great inspiration and enhanced creativity (Buenaflor, *Curanderismo Soul Retieval*, 42).

On spiritual and soul levels, ceremonies that inspire us to be positive, present, engaged, and grateful are food for the spirit and soul. Of course, for those who have been in prolonged negative mental or emotional states, these positive effects may not occur right away. Nevertheless, with these rites we rewire ourselves to experience more positive states, such as gratitude. For example, rites that remind us to approach the sun as a divine entity emitting sacred essence energy reinforces a sense of magic and beauty in our lives.

Approaching life as a sacred ceremonial dance of remembrance and gratitude may be difficult at first, but it gets easier with further practice. It is well worth the effort.

## WORKING WITH SOLAR AND LUNAR PHASES

My curanderx mentors taught me that the moon generally emits magical energies, while the sun gives off sacred essence energy. In order to garner the power of these forces, I always consider the phases of both the moon and sun before engaging in any ceremony. I always try to work with the phase that best suits my intention. But if there is a need for an immediate rite and the phase is not ideal, I will word my invocation to utilize the current phase. For instance, if I am intending to ensure success in a new venture (something more fitting for the new moon) or continuing success in a current venture (something that is better suited to the waxing moon) and these phases are not occurring, then I ask to transmute, with and by the sacred fires of God's love and light, everything and anything that may in any way, shape, or form obstruct or impede the ideal new . . . or continuing success of . . . I may also connect with the ideal phase by sending love to the sun or moon and visualizing this phase in my mind's eye, knowing that the connection has been made.

I am more apt to do a night ceremony, working with the night sun, if transformation is an underlying intent (or if I am guided to do so) and to work with the day sun if I wish to boost my intentions with its power (or again, if I am guided to do so). Whether it is day or night, I always consider the phase of the moon. I believe the moon is very much awake during the day and always work with it to infuse my intentions with its sacred magic. The energies of both sun and moon will always influence each other, and I always take into consideration what this may look like.

I also want to stress my love for both the sun and the moon. I have allotted more chapters to the sun for two principal reasons. First, the Mexica and many of the ancient Maya organized their day and related rites based on the sun rather than the moon. Common people experienced each of the divisions or phases of both the sun and night sun, and engaged in related rites, on a daily basis, while they only experienced phases of the moon on certain days of their solar months. Although indigenous peoples like the Otomis of Central Mexico and the Maya women of Cozumel did adore the moon (probably even more than the sun), they still organized their predominant division of rites and practices around the sun.

It is important to keep in mind that Mesoamerican peoples manipulated concepts of time or improvised new ways of looking—such as the beginning of a day or the number of lunar cycles in a calendar—to suit local agendas.[33] The southern Maya Lowlands, for example, in approximately 682 CE, adopted a uniform lunar calendar wherein independent cities numbered the moons or age of the moon and position of the moon in the lunar calendar exactly the same.[34] Prior to 682, there was no uniformity as to the numbering and position of the moons in a lunar calendar. Mesoamerican scholar John Teeple asserts that this apparent uniformity likely had to with politics and conquest.[35] Although there were diverse and multivalent expressions and understandings of time in ancient Mesoamerica, there were nonetheless mythological themes and meanings related to these phases that were resilient and could be traced throughout many regions, cultures, and periods of ancient Mesoamerica. This book reflects the likely predominate quadripartite division of their day, with the sun as the principal reference point.

Furthermore, our understanding of the rites associated with the phases of the moon among the ancient Mesoamerican peoples is still in its incipience. A phenomenal amount of work has been done to track, study, and understand the solar hierophanies, while research on lunar hierophanies pales in comparison. Much of the Lunar Series, which I discuss in chapter 7, still needs to be deciphered. Perhaps in years to come, when more research has been done, I will write another edition that will expand on ancient Mesoamerican lunar phases and rites, and on how we may benefit from this sacred wisdom.

# 1

# Intertwining the Energies of the Sun and Moon

## *The Sacred in Ancient Mexica and Maya Daily Life*

Spirituality, politics, and popular culture were highly intertwined in ancient Mesoamerica, and these belief systems were closely tied to celestial phenomena, particularly the movements and locations of the sun and moon and their interactions with other celestial phenomena. The shamans and nobles that performed celestial observations kept track of the length of the solar year, the lunar month, and the periods of revolution of Venus. They also charted the annual movement of the sunrise and sunset along the horizon and other celestial cycles.[1]

Celestial observations were multifaceted in purpose and meaning. They influenced economic, agricultural, and political activities; rituals related to seasonal and agricultural cycles; divinatory advents; and the creation and reinforcement of social and political identities.

Beliefs about the patterns, movements, and energies of the sun and moon were embedded in the culture of the Mesoamericans. They divided the universe into a horizontally quadripartite form, ordered in four cardinal spaces with a center in the middle, and a vertically tripartite form, with the Underworld, Middleworld, and Upperworld. For both the Mexica and Maya, the sun and moon were both part of the Upperworld. Each cardinal space had its own particular sacred essence energies, divine wisdom, sacred gifts, patrons, colors, World Trees, and mountains, and these were perceived as both fixed and unfixed metaphorical spaces.[2]

The quadripartite pattern was portrayed as a quincunx, one of the most common geometrical forms, with its four directions plus a point in the center. This pattern was mirrored in Mesoamerican city designs, causeways, temples, homes, plazas, and other ritual spaces.[3] This quadripartite division was associated with the sun's annual and daily movements. Annually, the sun had four primary solstitial movements and points—two on the east and two on the west; the central point represented the intersection of the paths marking the yearly movement of the sun. Daily, the sun also had four primary movements, spaces, and divisions: the points of sunrise and sunset and zenith and nadir.[4]

The Mesoamericans' general principal measurements of time also reflected a quadripartite division. Their Calendar Round supported a religious system that linked the heavens with seasonal cycles and the agricultural rituals associated with them.[5] The calendar was composed of two calendars: the solar calendar (20 days and 18 periods, with 5 liminal days at the end of the year: a total of 365 days) and a ritual calendar (20 day signs that reigned over 13 days: a total of 260 days). These would synchronize with each other over a period of 52 years. These 52 years were divided into four 13-year periods, each of which was oriented to a cardinal space with its own distinct energies, divine beings, meanings, and rituals. The four divisions were also expressed in the ritual calendar: each of its 20 days came under the influence of one of the four cardinal spaces, with their own distinct energies and meanings.[6]

Each of the quadripartite divisions of the day emitted different sacred energies and required particular offerings and ceremonies.[7] This quadripartite division in turn included further subdivisions, nuancing the energies of each period and requiring their own particular rites.

Mesoamerican creation myths typically involve two mythical beings that were resurrected as the sun and the moon, sometimes after the performance of a heroic deed. Although rituals do not necessarily replicate the core mythical creation themes in every detail, the importance of these themes was apparent in government, spirituality, and culture. Buildings were often oriented to display solar and lunar hierophanies that empowered rituals and supported the legitimacy of rulers and nobles. Sacred items were believed to be imbued with energies from the sun and moon.

## THE SUN AND MOON OF THE ANCIENT MEXICA

The Mexica divided their days into four principal parts, which emanated distinct energies: sunrise to noon, known as Iquiza-Tonatiuh; noon to sunset, Nepantla-Tonatiuh; sunset to midnight, Oaqui-Tonatiuh; and midnight to sunrise, Yohualnepantla. The midquarters of these four divisions, and the periods leading up to them, were also symbolically and ritually significant and had their own discrete energies.[8]

In many rituals celebrating their deities, the Mexica offered incense according to these divisions and subdivisions. In the Nahui Ollin (four-motion) rite,* their feast to honor the sun, they offered incense to an

*Sahagún, in *Primeros Memoriales,* asserts that the Mexica honored the sun five times: (1) dawn, (2) midmorning, (3) high noon, when the sun was at the highest altitude in the sky, (4) midday, and (5) sunset (Sahagún, *Primeros Memoriales,* 153). But there is more evidence that the sun was honored by the state four times a day. In the *Florentine Codex,* Sahagún himself states that the Mexica honored the sun four times in the day: dawn, midmorning, midday (likely high noon), and sunset (Sahagún, *Florentine Codex,* 2:216). Muñoz Camargo, the sixteenth-century ethnographer of the Tlaxcala, also records four times when the sun was honored: dawn, midmorning, noon, and sunset (Muñoz Camargo, *Historia de Tlaxcala,* 159). The discrepancies may be due to annual seasonal changes or different linguistic interpretations. The Mexica knew when it was midnight by looking at the planets, which appeared to change positions throughout the night and seasons.

image of the sun depicted as a butterfly in a golden circle, emitting radiant beams and glowing lines. This ritual took place four times a day: sunrise, noon, past midday, and sunset.[9] For the feasts of Xochiquetzal, Huitzilopochtli, and others, they also offered incense to the images four times a day.[10]

At nighttime, after the festival of Nahui Ollin, the Mexica greeted the night sun and offered incense to it four times. They also offered incense to the constellations that marked the four cardinal points in the sky: Yohualitqui Mamalhuaztli (Orion's Belt; also the name they gave to the sticks with which they drilled fire); Citlalthachtli (a celestial ball court, possibly Gemini and other stars to its right); Colotl Ixayac (the Scorpion); and Tianquitztli (the Pleiades). This ritual took place: (1) when it was becoming dark and Yohualitqui Mamalhuaztli was visible (2) when it was completely dark; (3) at bedtime, around 10 p.m.; (4) when Tianquitztli reached its zenith and the trumpets were sounded, slightly before midnight; (5) at midnight; (6) when Venus as the Morning Star appeared; and (7) when it began to dawn and the Morning Star took the place of the Pleiades.[11]

On a daily basis, the Mexica sounded the trumpets and offered incense to the sun at: (1) dawn; (2) midmorning; (3) high noon, when the sun was at the highest altitude in the sky; (4) midday (likely afternoon); and (5) sunset.[12] At night, they offered incense and played trumpets as follows: (1) at nightfall; (2) when it was time to go to sleep, around 10 p.m.; (3) slightly before midnight; (4) at midnight; and (5) near dawn.[13] The sounding of temple drums and conches also marked slightly different times for ritual activities: (1) sunrise; (2) midmorning; (3) noon; (4) sunset; (5) the end of the twilight at the beginning of night, (6) around 10 p.m.; (7) a little before midnight; (8) a little after midnight; and (9) a little before dawn.[14]

The Mexica believed the sun was the principal source of sacred essence energy. They divided space and time according to the quadripartite solar cycles and performed divination concerning the sun principally at the points of the annual and daily cycles and at its interaction with other celestial bodies. At sunrise, the sun was accompanied by the souls of brave warriors; then, after its zenith (at high noon), it was accompanied by the souls of brave warrior women who died during childbirth. At sunset, the sun began its journey through the dangerous levels of the Underworld. Xolotl, under his guise as Tlalchitonatiuh, was able to exit and enter the Underworld and guided the sun through the Underworld to be reborn each morning in the east. Emerging out of the west reflected a transformative interrelationship between the processes of decay, death, germination, fertility, renewal, and rebirth.[15] Mexica ball courts reflected the narrow passageway of the Underworld, through which the sun traveled at night. Competing factions played out a cosmic struggle to see which group could bring the sun out of the Underworld by hitting the ball through one of the two perforated rings on the sides of the court.[16]

The Mexica believed that the moon (*metzli*) was awake at night and slept during the day. They looked to the appearance of the moon and its alignment with other celestial bodies for divinatory and magical purposes. They believed that a red moon was a sign of heat, a bright red moon indicated dry temperature, a white moon signaled cold temperature, and a yellow or golden moon referred to water, likely rain. When the tips of the crescent moon pointed to the north, it was an indication of coming rain; when the tips of the crescent moon pointed to the south, it was an indication of heat. A white ring around the moon pointed to a bad omen, while a colored ring around it was a good omen, marking a good time for commencing activities.[17] The Xaltocan, who became a part of the Aztec empire in 1395, were avid worshipers of the moon, which was one of their principal deities.[18]

The Mexica typically divided their Upperworld into thirteen realms, although a few sources indicate a division of nine or twelve.[19] Vatican Codex A describes the levels of the Upperworld. The lowest one was visible to all; it was the realm where the moon and clouds traveled. The second level was Citlalco, the place of the stars.[20] The third level was the one in which Tonatiuh, the sun deity, resided.[21] The rest of the levels were occupied by comets, storms, and the dwelling places of deities.[22]

The Mexica performed calculations to determine meteorological activity and to predict eclipses. The people of the Aztec empire greatly feared lunar and solar eclipses, which were believed to be bad portents, signaling destruction. During a lunar eclipse, when the moon is full, the most affected were pregnant women. They would place an obsidian knife on their bellies or in their mouths if they went out at night during this time. It was believed that if a pregnant woman went out at night and saw an eclipse of the moon, she would give birth to a baby with a harelip or might miscarry.[23]

Solar eclipses, which occur when there is a new moon, were dangerous for everyone; people would weep and shout.[24] The *tzitzimime,* star demons of the night sky, could also descend to wreak havoc among mortals.[25] The Mexica likened the death of a ruler to the onset of a solar eclipse and the subsequent installation of a new ruler to the sun's reappearance after darkness, reflecting a belief that rulers had the ability to renew the world and reenact the birth of the sun.[26]

The creation mythology of the sun and moon, as noted by the Florentine Codex and the *Leyenda de los soles* (legend of the suns), concerned two beings that resurrected into the sun and moon. The Mexica believed that prior to their current world, there had been four prior worlds or suns, each named by a date in their ritual calendar and identified with a particular deity and race of humans.[27] The creation of their fifth sun took place at Teotihuacan, when all was in darkness and there was no sun or moon. The deities gathered there to see who would offer themselves to be the sun. Tecuciztecatl, a wealthy deity, as indicated by the costly and extravagant offerings he made, presented himself. No one else offered themselves accept Nanahuatzin, a humbler deity sometimes described as being covered in pustules.

For four days, they fasted and made offerings. Then, at midnight, all the gods encircled the hearth or fire called *teotexcalli,* where they were expected to offer themselves to raise the sun. When it came time for Tecuciztecatl to throw himself into the hearth, he found the heat intolerable, and he could not. Four times he tried but was unsuccessful. He called to Nanahuatzin to throw himself into the fire. Nanahuatzin had no fear and did so; he was resurrected as Tonatiuh, the fiery sun god who rises in the east. Tecuciztecatl, embarrassed, threw himself into the fire and rose up. Because of his cowardice, one of the deities threw a rabbit into his face and darkened his shine, and he became the moon.[28] The moon was considered to be a replica of the sun.[29]

The relationship between the sun and moon reflected the Mexica's belief in divine opposing pairs, dynamic feminine-masculine dyads that were fundamental to the creation, regeneration, and sustenance of the cosmos.[30] This spiritual belief was reflected in their political structure, where the *huey tlatoani* (great ruler), head of the Aztec empire and military and supreme judge, was often associated with sun deities.[31] At the huey tlatoani's side was the *cihuacoatl* (woman serpent or feminine twin), who discharged the duties of the huey tlatoani in his absence. The cihuacoatl was head of the civil service and police, supervised the collection of taxes and tributes, and parceled out the land. He was also the priest of the deity Cihuacoatl, who was associated with the moon, possibly the new moon and the solar eclipse, and was a part of the Teteo innan complex of Earth fertility deities.[32]

The huey tlatoani's association with the heroic sun deities and his ability to connect with and have the support of the sun was exhibited in Mexica public monuments and in ritual displays of solar hierophanies. Mesoamerican scholar David Stuart suggests that the image in the middle of the twelve-foot Sun Stone of Tenochtitlan was likely a defied portrayal of Moctezuma II, the huey tlatoani at the time of Hernán Cortés's arrival to the Aztec empire in 1519. It is not a conventional portrait of Moctezuma but depicts him as a mythological figure embodying various divine beings and cosmic elements and associated with the personification of time.[33]

The smaller rays are solar rays; the larger four surrounding the Nahui Ollin refer to the four cardinal directions, as well as to previous creations, marking the Ollin as the world center. The face of the Ollin sign is the animate visage of both terrestrial and celestial movement, and possibly the sun's reflection on or within the Earth.[34] The glyphs between the middle ray of the Ollin above the face, Stuart suggests, also have a direct connection with its identities. The leftmost hieroglyph, the Xocotl glyph, represents both the dead warriors who accompany the sun at sunrise and Moctezuma II with a royal *xuihuitzolli* headband, opposite a calendrical reference to 1 Flint (*ce tecpatl*), the birth date of Huitzilopochtli.[35]

Durán states that the Sun Stone represents Moctezuma I at high noon.[36] Mesoamerican scholar Karl Taube asserts that the Sun Stone also illustrated the fiery birth of the sun and the sun at full glory in the center of the sky and was a dynamic portrayal of transformation and resurrection. The image in the middle is likely conflated with the following sun deities and rulers: Tonatiuh, the sun deity of the fifth world; the night sun, Yohualtecuhtli; and Huitzilopochtli as the sun in its zenith with a flint-knife tongue, possibly alluding to the fifth and sixth rulers of the Mexica, Moctezuma I and II.[37] These representations indicated that the supreme head was connected with and able to embody cosmic elements and actions along with different sun deities in their most prestigious aspects.

The huey tlatoani and his advisors also used hierophanies in their architecture to illuminate and reiterate their spiritual and political beliefs and intertwine them into and bolster their power and legitimacy. The Great Temple of Tenochtitlan, the Templo Mayor, mirrored the axis mundi, the point of intersection of all the world's paths, both terrestrial and celestial. It was the center of the world and of the four cardinal spaces. Its four steplike platforms on top of one another relate to the cardinal quadrants, as does the courtyard, with its four doors or entrances at the east, west, north, and south, each of which was named after the deity of its cardinal direction. The three lower platforms consisted of 12 sections; the 13th section was the small top platform, where the dual temples of Huitzilopochtli and Tlaloc were located; these 13 sections mirrored and acted as a gateway to the 13 levels of the Upperworld.[38] The architects designed the temple at 7 degrees and 6 minutes to the south of a true east-west line so that the sun could be seen at dawn on the day of the equinox as it rose between the temples of Huitzilopochtli and Tlaloc.[39] This brilliant manifestation of the sun at dawn empowered, for example, the later appearance of Toci by the *teccizquacuilli* (shaman performer), at their state-sponsored rite, Ochpaniztli (sweeping the way).

Malinalco, a city located east of Tenochtitlan, was incorporated into the Aztec empire in 1469–76. The temples of Malinalco are sculptured. They were carved into a sloping hill oriented toward the southeast in order to garner the sacred essence energy of the sun. Temple IV of Malinalco faces east and is considered to be a sun temple. The temple wall was designed to receive the light rays of the rising sun and has an image of the sun similar to the Sun Stone embedded into it.[40] This hierophany was likely enacted to animate and vivify the temple with sacred essence energy.

Charging sacred ritual tools and items with the sun's sacred essence energy was also done during the eleventh month of their ritual calendar, *tonalpohualli*. The Mexica brought forth the sacred ornaments of Huitzilopochtli, cleaned them, and placed them in the sun to be charged with *tonalli* (sacred essence energy or soul energy).[41] The Mexica also engaged in ritual sunbathing to garner tonalli.

## THE SUN OF THE ANCIENT MAYA

Friar Diego de Landa, a sixteenth-century missionary and ethnographer, states, "During the day they [Yucatec Maya] had terms for midday, and for different sections from sunrise to sunset, according to which they recognized and regulated their hours for work."[42] The Maya hieroglyph for *sun* and *day*, K'in, strongly suggests that they divided their day into four principal phases and periods that were centered around these phases. K'in equaled a day and referred to the sun. It embodied the sun's horizontal movement from east to west and vertical movement between up (north) and down (south). It was a signifier of time and a descriptor of space. The hieroglyph, with four petallike lobes, also represents the four world directions with a center.[43] Decipherments of carved inscriptions reveal that royal ceremonies and accessions often coincided with quadripartite stations of the sun.[44]

The Popol Vuh, a sixteenth-century K'iché' Maya work comprising creation myths, legends, history, and ethical teachings, also indicates that the sun's motion defines the four quarters of the universe. But this quadripartite division was actually set in place before the sun was created, when a cord was stretched in the sky and on Earth at the time of creation.[45] The sun god was also a patron of the number four, reflecting the understanding of this quadripartite division.[46]

The Upperworld of the ancient Maya, like that of the Mexica, was divided into thirteen distinct realms. According to the Chilam Balam* of Maní, the moon was in the first level and the sun was in the fourth. The Chilam Balam of Kaua also placed the sun in the fourth level.[47] In artwork, the sun and moon were often depicted along a double-headed serpent that represented the ecliptic and traced the annual motion of the sun across the sky. The double-headed serpent was referred to as *kan,* meaning both "sky" and "serpent" in Yucatec Mayan. The Maya looked to the astrological movements of the Upperworld to ascertain the will and activities of ancestors and deities.[48]

After sunset, one aspect of the sun deity was believed to shapeshift into a jaguar and roam the Underworld; another was carried through the Underworld by a centipede, which eventually released the sun at dawn in the east.[49] As a jaguar, the sun passed to the Underworld to become one of the Lords of Night.[50] The sun deity emerged from the Underworld at dawn with death markings, the attributes of a jaguar, and the color black.[51]

---

*The books of Chilam Balam are the sacred books of the Maya of Yucatán; they are the most important source on the traditional knowledge of the Maya and early Spanish traditions. They were handwritten and are named after the small Yucatec towns where they were originally kept.

The best-known Maya creation mythology of the sun and the moon is in the Popol Vuh. One of the principal stories relays the battles between two pairs of twins and the Lords of the Underworld, Xilbalba. The first set of twins is defeated by the lords, who cut off the head of Hun Hunahpu, one of the brothers. The lords hang his severed head like a trophy on a gourd tree. Xkik (Blood Moon Woman), a maiden of the Underworld, attracted by the gourds, reaches for one, and the spittle from the head of Hun Hunahpu impregnates her with the second generation of Hero Twins.[52] The second set of twins must also pass many tests and go through the different levels of Xilbalba.

After the Lords of the Underworld are defeated in a ball-court game, they invite the twins to jump over a fiery pit. Although they know that the lords only want them dead, they valiantly jump into the pit. The lords then grind up their charred bones and throw them into the river. In five days the twins are resurrected as fish-men and are invited before the lords to perform feats of resurrection. They trick the lords, who ask to be killed so they can be later resurrected. The twins kill one of them but leave him dead and lifeless. The twins defeat the lords, who beg for mercy and are told that they shall never be powerful again. After defeating the lords and recovering the remains of their father and uncle, the twins rise into the heavens to become the moon and the sun.[53]

In many other mythologies, the sun courts the moon, and they sometimes become a couple.[54] At Yaxchilan, a portrait of the ruler's mother is depicted within the lunar sign, while a portrait of the ruler's father is depicted within the solar sign. This pairing led many scholars to believe that the moon was the wife of the sun.[55]

The sun god was closely identified with elite rulership in both the Classic (250–909 CE) and Postclassic periods (909–1697 CE). Mayanist J. Eric S. Thompson asserts that the sun deity was always depicted in the auguries, or precontact Maya codices, in a malignant manner, with drought and bad weather. The sun was more dreaded than loved because unless the rain gods intervened, the sun would scorch the crops.[56] Certain aspects of the sun were feared, and the destruction of the crops was well recorded in the codices to prepare for or avoid future calamities from the sun. Elite classes nonetheless associated themselves with the sun god during their lives, and in some instances depicted their apotheosis at death resurrecting as the sun, or with the sun on the eastern horizon.[57]

An important title of Maya lords was *k'inich* (sun face).[58] Terms derived from K'in were also used to denote rulership and wealth in K'iché' and Yucatec Mayan. Tikal Stela 31 displays one of the clearest examples of Maya identification of the sun god with dynastic rulership.[59] It depicts the father of Classic ruler Stormy Sky as the sun god with the deity's Classical characteristics: Roman nose, squint eyes, jaguar spit cheek markings, and a sharply upcurving nose bar.[60] The sarcophagus lid of Classic ruler K'inich Janaab' Pakal I in Palenque, on the southern part of the Yucatán Peninsula, depicts his departure out of the Underworld and his resurrection, regeneration, and rebirth. The resurrected ruler rises up along a World Tree, which acts as an axis mundi or portal that transfers his body to a flowery realm in the Upperworld. Pakal wears the symbols of the sun god, and like the sun, he will be reborn at dawn.[61]

Solar, lunar, and stellar cartouches were frequently associated with ancestor spirits in Maya art, particularly on monuments from Yaxchilan. The Berlin Vase illustrates a burial scene of a soul undergoing a solar ascent. A solar cartouche rises above the bundled corpse with his forehead shown as a burning *ajaw* face. (The ajaw face was often depicted with two dots as the eyes, and a third dot at the bottom as the mouth.) The back of the sun god's head is marked by a moon sign floating before the glyph *bih* (road), depicting the deceased entering the celestial path of the souls. Solar and lunar ascent were popular tropes among the Maya.[62]

Eclipses were seen as the biting of the sun or moon or a monster devouring the sun.[63] The Maya created tables in their codices to warn of eclipses.[64] To them, solar eclipses were more dangerous than lunar eclipses. In the Dresden Codex, a solar eclipse was typically pictured as the eating of the K'in glyph by a sky serpent. Predicting eclipses was essential, because it enabled the Maya to engage in rituals to prevent disasters caused by them.[65] The Chilam Balam of Chumayel describes an apocalyptic event during a five-day solar eclipse. Eclipses coincided with periods of transition and liminality, marking the end of particular intervals of time.[66]

Solar and lunar architectural hierophanies infused state-sponsored and private ceremonies with sacred cosmic significance. The performer, sacred tool, or site would be imbued with cosmic sacred essence, facilitating an apotheosis or rebirth, or the embodiment of a deity.

While the research into lunar hierophanies and related rituals is not as extensive as for solar ones, it is forthcoming. The Cross Group buildings (the Temples of the Cross, Foliated Cross, and Sun) at Classic Palenque were interrelatedly aligned to the sun and moon, so that the sun, moon, solar rays, or their alignments were commemorated by critical imperial rites. The Cross Group also represents shrines to the three patron deities of Palenque, GI, GII, and GIII and contains tablets with texts that connected the reign of ruler Kan B'ahlam II with these gods of creation.[67] The longitudinal axis of the Temple of the Cross (119 degrees east–301 degrees west) coincides with the maximum excursions of the moon. The moon rising at its maximum southern extreme on the eastern horizon would not have been visible from the central doorway of the Temple of the Sun but would have been seen setting over the roof comb of the Temple of the Sun from the Temple of the Foliated Cross.[68] Imperial shamanic rites were likely performed by Kan B'ahlam II on both new- and full-moon phases to garner their sacred energies and legitimize his reign.[69]

Many lunar architectural hierophanies have also been found in the northeastern part of the Yucatán Peninsula, including the island of Cozumel.[70] During the Postclassic period, Cozumel was an important focus of worship of the moon deity, Ix Chel. Women conducted pilgrimages to worship Ix Chel, whom de Landa identified as a deity of the moon, childbirth, and medicine.[71] While most of the hierophanies on Cozumel can be related to the sun, many of the orientations correspond to the standstills or extremes of the moon.[72]

Numerous solar hierophanies—manifested as plays of light/shadow, solar illumination, and interbuilding solar alignments—have been studied in the Maya region.[73] One of the first examples of an architectural hierophany is in the Group E complex at Early Classic Uaxactún, where solstice and equinox sunrises can be observed from a western structure facing three structures on the east side.[74] Group E complexes, which are a fairly common architectural layout, contain a single temple used for sighting that stands directly west of three buildings, each of which mark the winter solstice, summer solstice, and equinoxes. They cannot be considered genuine observatories, because they were not used to obtain new astronomical information.[75] At Chichén Itzá, the northwest staircase balustrades of the Temple of Kukulkan were carved with feathered serpents at the bottom. On the afternoon of the equinoxes, a shadow appears on the side of the staircase showing the serpent descending the steps to the plaza.[76]

At Palenque, the Temple of the Sun is oriented to face the rising sun at winter solstice, so that a ruler standing in the main doorway would have been fully illuminated by the public at the plaza, imbuing royal power with sacred essence energy.[77] The setting sun of the winter solstice sends a shaft of light coming from behind the Temple of the Inscriptions that slowly mounts the terraces of the Temple of the Cross; as the base of the pyramid sinks into shadow, a final beam of light enters the temple and illuminates God L on the eastern sanctuary doorjamb.[78] God L was a wealthy god of trade, tribute, and tobacco. Although he has been traditionally associated with the Underworld, he was able to leave it and traverse both the Middleworld and the first levels of the Upperworld, often as the personification of Venus.[79] The hierophany likely represents the successful transfer of power of Janaab'

Pakal to his son and heir Kan B'ahlam II under the auspices of God L. This transfer is displayed on the tablet at the Temple of Cross (or is at least one of its many meanings).[80] Since God L crossed into and out of the different levels of nonordinary realms, it is likely that he may have assisted Janaab' Pakal in the transfer of power.

# 2

# Mesoamerican Solar and Lunar Deities

## *Reflections of Sacred Energies*

The manners in which ancient Mexica and Maya understood and represented their deities served as models and metaphors of their social and natural worlds.[1] Certain deities were associated with phases of the moon; daily and annual movements of the sun; cosmic alignments of the sun and the moon; and their traits. The genders and ages of these deities were not static elements. The embodiment, performance, or use of such elements was essential in ensuring the success of their rites.

The age of solar deities often correlated with the seasons, the sun's daily and annual movements, and other cosmic interactions. Solar deities were typically depicted as male. This lent itself to beliefs about brave male warriors who died on the battlefield and whose souls would later rise with the sun in the east to spend the afterlife in a paradisal Flower World. Although women were not explicitly excluded from military institutions, they generally did not serve as warriors.[2]

The genders of moon deities were much more complex and polysemic. The moon was associated with vegetation, water, earth, and by extension the powers of procreation and regeneration—processes and qualities to which many rulers and nobles, both male and female, wanted to be connected with.[3] The moon deities' association with bodies of water stemmed from the belief that an aspect of this deity resided in the Upperworld of Tlalocan, the fertile paradisal realm of the rain gods and those who died by water.[4] Again, the age of moon deities corresponded with the phases of the moon and other celestial interactions.

This chapter surveys a sample of the different solar and lunar deities and some of the sacred costuming, tools, and accoutrements with which they were associated. Understanding the elements of these solar and lunar rites can bolster the potency of our own rites, whether through the intentions we set out or through the details of the ceremonies.

## MEXICA SOLAR DEITIES

One of the best known solar deities of the Mexica is Tonatiuh. As noted in the previous chapter, Nanahuatzin was resurrected into Tonatiuh after he valiantly threw himself into the fiery hearth. Tonatiuh was equated with solar forces and movements, including radiating heat energy and tonalli.[5] Tonalli was an animating sacred energy that diffused over and energized the Earth and its inhabitants and was essential to life. It was absorbed by animals, plants, fire, statues, gemstones, brilliantly colored bird feathers, animal skins, warrior's costumes, and mats woven with *mallinalli* grass. Tonalli was associated with sustenance, ripening, and renewal.[6] Like the ritual performers who embodied deities and could transmit *teyolia,* the sacred energy of the heart, to their communities during ceremonies and speeches, shamans of high rank, nobles, and rulers were able to emit sweet, strong, and revitalizing tonalli to the people.[7]

Every day Tonatiuh rose from the east with the brave warriors who died in war and made its way to its zenith at high noon. The souls of these warriors were transformed into birds, butterflies, and hummingbirds and were said to live in eternal happiness.[8] The sun, Tonatiuh, was also connected with butterflies and birds, particularly hummingbirds.[9]

Granting the title of eagle or jaguar was a great honor given to brave warriors.[10] This identification with the eagle and jaguar likely comes from the *Leyenda de los soles* (legend of the suns). After Nanahuatzin threw himself into the fiery hearth, the jaguar went into the hearth but was not able to carry him out and became spotted from the fire. Then the hawk made the attempt but was smoked. The wolf also tried and was scorched. The eagle, however, was able to carry him out of the fire, and Nanahuatzin rose up to become the sun, Tonatiuh. Sacred eagle paraphernalia relayed courage—the courage needed to rise with the sun. While jaguars are often depicted with solar deities, this may allude to a different solar deity or a different aspect, one involving the sun's journey through the Underworld at night.[11]

Tonatiuh was typically depicted with eagle accoutrements, a red-painted body, red or yellow face paint, a semicircle as a ridge embracing both eyes, a jeweled nose rod, yellow hair, golden bird fillet, fire sticks as part of his headdress, and a sun insignia that radiated heat energy (see plate 1).[12] He was also portrayed as a butterfly in a golden circle emitting radiant beams.[13]

At the height of the sun's power at high noon, it was associated with Huitzilopochtli, the tutelary war deity of the Mexica who guided them from their original home in Aztlan to their promised land in the Valley of Mexico, Tenochtitlan.[14] He often wore a blue-green hummingbird headdress; carried the Xiuhcoatl, a fire serpent that was used as a weapon and a mirror; and had on his back an *anecuyotl* (possibly a backpack, sometimes bearing the insignia of his drunken and defeated half brothers, *centzonuitznaua*).[15] He sometimes had a black face, and his body was painted blue or had yellow and blue stripes. He was known to appear as a celestial fire, a snake, or a hummingbird.[16] As the beloved Mexica war deity, he epitomized valor, courage, and strength.

Tlalchitonatiuh (sun going into earth) was the setting sun as it descends in the west. Tlalchitonatiuh is the partner of Xolotl, who guides the nighttime sun along its eastward journey through the Underworld so it may exit and be reborn. Page 16 of the Codex Borbonicus depicts Xolotl facing Tlalchitonatiuh, who is displayed in a mortuary bundle with fangs and a sun insignia in the middle of his body. His eye has been removed and apparently placed on his forehead; a night eye insignia is on top of his head; an arrow sticking out of his mouth indicates his death; and he is being devoured by the maws of earth (see plate 2).[17] The death of the sun deity was closely connected with rebirth. The *trecena* (13-day) sign of Xolotl is a vulture, who eats dead flesh, transforming life into death.[18] On page 35 of the Codex Borgia, Tlalchitonatiuh is an elderly black being with Tonatiuh's facial markings and wearing a crocodile skin with a large red sphere at the belly.

Another solar deity was Xochipilli (flower prince), who was associated with the youthful sun, young corn, flowers, poetry, butterflies, fertility, the rainy season of the year, and the rising sun at dawn.[19] His attributes typically included a red parrot helmet, yellow or red face paint, white around the mouth, a jeweled nose bar and a bird-headed fillet, both associated with solar gods.[20] In the central highlands of Mexico, the rainy season runs from May to the end of October, and the dry season runs from November through April. The dry season was a time for ritual warfare and long-distance trade.

Mesoamerican scholar Susan Milbrath posits that Xochipilli, in a flower temple, appears on page 42 of the Codex Borgia at the fall equinox in September, and on page 37 at the summer solstice (see plate 3). Solar deities appear in flowered temples on pages that correspond to the summer solstice and the fall equinox; that is, the rainy season.[21] Flowered borders and temples with flowers on the roof are present only on pages correlating with the rainy season, as well as bees, bee deities, bats, butterflies, and hummingbirds.[22]

Other deities were depicted with solar sacred tools and accessories. The female deity Chicomecoatl (Seven Snake), associated with corn, agriculture, and sustenance, was often depicted as carrying a shield with a sun symbol.[23] The Macuiltonaleque, five young solar deities associated with tempering excess pleasure, lust, and gambling, also often wore sandals with a sun insignia.[24]

## MEXICA LUNAR DEITIES

Mexica moon deities could be portrayed as solely male or female, but could also have a third-gender aspect. They were often depicted with lunar accessories, such as a nose ornament in the form of a lunar crescent or a crescent headdress.[25]

Numerous scholars have identified the aged deity, Toci, also known as Teteo innan as a lunar being.[26] The third-gender aspects of Toci seem to have been invoked at the peak of transformative, regenerative, and generative processes, such as seasonal transitions. Her feminine aspects were related to regenerative and generative cycles, while her idealized masculine aspects alluded to strength and virility. The symbols and activities associated with Toci could either literally or metaphorically relate to both males and females.[27] Toci's transformative abilities could be invoked by fashioning her symbolic garments or tools and by engaging in activities associated with Toci. Toci was associated with spinning, weaving, sweeping, divination, illicit sexual union, childbirth, and acting as a protector and warrior.[28] Both Sahagún and Durán say Toci holds a broom in one hand and a warrior's shield in the other. Toci's headdress is either a crescent with bunches of unspun cotton or spindle whorls with bunches of spun and unspun cotton and a star skirt.[29]

Xochiquetzal (Precious Flower or Flower Quetzal), another deity associated with the Teteo innan complex, is often identified as a lunar deity.[30] In her feminine aspect, she is a young deity associated with the arts, passionate love, sexual power and the sexual arts, and flowers. She was a patroness of weavers, featherworking, painting, sculpting, metalworking, healing, and divination, and she presided over pregnancy and childbirth.[31] Xochiquetzal's ritual instruments included the weaving spindle and batten, the sweat bath, flowers, and butterflies.[32] Her attire included twin feathered plumes, a quetzal helmet, flowers in a headdress, jeweled face ornamentations, a curved jade nose ornament, elaborately embroidered woven skirts, and the weaving batten.[33] According to Mesoamerican scholar Thelma D. Sullivan, Aztec state imagery depicting Xochiquetzal menacingly with a weaving batten in her hands is meant to identify her with other woman warrior deities.[34]

Xochiquetzal's third-gender aspects were invoked to utilize her transformative abilities. This aspect made an appearance during the Pachtontli rite, marking a seasonal transition and ensuring the return of the flowers. At the point of the flowers' death, Xochiquetzal appeared through a *tlamacazque* (male shaman), who donned both the male and female aspects of Xochiquetzal.[35] Xochiquetzal sat at the steps of the Templo Mayor and was given a weaving loom to weave the rejuvenation of flowers and the fate of the Aztec empire. A relief from Ixtapalulca shows her wearing a female skirt with a male loincloth.[36]

Cihuacoatl was a deity who was also associated with the Teteo innan complex. As a lunar deity, Cihuacoatl embodied the creative power of the Earth and sometimes had malevolent traits, destroying life, particularly during an eclipse.[37] Cihuacoatl has also been depicted as a skeletal old woman, Ilamatecuhutli (Old Woman Lord).[38] As mentioned, Cihuacoatl was also the title of one of the highest governing positions held by males who handled the internal affairs of the state. In some of Cihuacoatl's pictorial representations, Cihuacoatl is fearsome, bearing a shield and spear, and has a snake, which is believed to represent a penis that is coming out of the tunic.[39] Cihuacoatl was associated with activities such as midwifery, healing, purification, and acting as a protector and warrior. Cihuacoatl's symbols included bear spears, the shield, the sweat bath, and the weaving batten.[40] Cihuacoatl was sometimes painted gold above the waist and red below and had wild hair with banners of flags.[41]

Cihuacoatl's transformative, generative, and regenerative nature could be invoked to cause and direct cyclical successions.[42] During the Tititl rite, which marked the end of the cold and frost, Cihuacoatl's third-gender aspect, along with the complementary male and female aspects, made an appearance, principally to secure an auspicious seasonal transition.[43] Cihuacoatl's feminine, masculine, and third-gender aspects were dressed almost identically: a starched white skirt and shirt; a white girdle over garments that had long strips of cured skin with shells at the end of each strip (these jingled loudly in the acoustically rich precinct of the Templo Mayor); and a shield in one hand and a weaving batten in the other. The toes were painted white, and each toe was woven with a cotton thread; the face was surreally painted in diverse colors.[44] The third-gender aspect began with the *ilamatecuhololoya* (Ilamatechtli's leap) dance, denoting an inversion. Then the shamans placed a mask on Cihucoatl that looked in two directions, had large lips, and a row of small flags on top.[45] Cihucoatl was now in her third-gender embodiment.

Tlazolteotl, known as the Great Spinner and Weaver or the Filth Deity, was also associated with the moon, platicas (heart-straightening talks), limpia sweeping rites, fertility and childbirth, menses, the steam bath, purification, sexuality, witchcraft, healing, and sexual misdeeds. She forgave, absolved sins, and healed illnesses.[46] She was believed to remove people's impurities during the platica, while her earthly diviners were responsible for listening and inquiring. Before death, it was common to summon a *tlapouhqui,* a shaman of Tlazolteotl skilled in reading and interpreting the sacred books, so that the dying person could confess all wrongdoings.[47] Tlazolteotl was also typically involved in healing illnesses related to sex.[48] Tlazolteotl is often depicted with a black area around the mouth, carrying a grass broom, wearing a headdress with weaving spindles, and wearing ear ornaments of unspun cotton.[49]

Another well-known moon deity is the defeated Coyolxuahqui, Lady of the Golden Bells, sister of the solar deity Huitzilopochtli. Her defeat was due to her alleged plot to kill her mother, Coatlique, after learning that she had become pregnant with Huitzilopochtli. Huitzilopochtli was born either after his mother's death or just in time to save Coatlique from Coyolxuahqui and their four hundred brothers. When he was born, he killed most of the brothers, cut off Coyolxauhqui's head, and threw it into the sky. Coyolxuahqui's head became the moon. Some scholars also claim that she is a moon deity because of the symbols on her head: hair adorned with feathers, earplugs in the form of the fire god, and golden bells made of metal on her cheeks.[50] She is only depicted in stone art. Her costume and iconography are, however, reminiscent of Chantico, deity of the hearth and patron of Xochimilco, who is only depicted in codices.[51] Although it would seem that Chantico would be solely associated with femininity and cooking because of her connection with the hearth, she is sometimes depicted with both a man's loincloth and a young woman's short skirt.[52]

## MAYA SOLAR DEITIES

For the Classic and Postclassic Maya, iconographic and epigraphic illustrations suggest that there were multiple solar deities, likely representing different aspects of the sun. For the most part, Classic and Postclassic representations of the Sun Deity (aka God G) are very similar.[53] Centipedes were often associated with the newly born sun as it emerged daily out of the Underworld and appear as his headdress; the corners of solar cartouches have four centipede heads.[54]

The diurnal sun deity, K'inich Ahau (Sun-Faced Lord or Sun-Eyed Lord), was often depicted with a bearded chin; a four-petaled K'in sign decorating his brow or body; a Roman nose; a large square eye (sometimes he is depicted in frontal view as cross-eyed); and snakelike curves extending from the mouth, often with his upper incisors filed into a T shape *ik'* (air or wind) sign, referring to the sacred essence energy that he emits.[55] The Classic Maya sun god was often portrayed with a centipede headdress.[56] He resembles a younger version of the aged creator deity, Itzamna, of whom he is an aspect—K'inich Ahau Itzamna. One of the most distinctive traits that sets K'inich Ahau apart from Itzamna is the K'in sign on his brow or body.[57] At the temple of K'inich Kakmo on the north side of the plaza of Izamal, it was said that the sun deity became a macaw to partake of, or burn, the offerings that have been left for him. On page 40b of the Dresden Codex, the god has a macaw head and human body carrying a burning torch, a symbol of drought or burning heat.[58]

Structure 16 at Postclassic Tulúm alludes to the Mayas' honoring two distinct sun deities, Tonatiuh and K'inich Ahau. One has solar rays and the headband of the Mexica sun deity, Tonatiuh. The other has a beard and is wearing a plumed serpent headdress, likely K'inich Ahau.[59] De Landa noted that mothers tried to make their sons cross-eyed, as it was believed to be a blessing; they would also burn their faces with hot cloths to prevent the growth of beards.[60] These acts likely relate to honoring both sun deities.

During the night, the sun deity journeyed through the Underworld in his manifestation as the fearsome Jaguar God.[61] The Jaguar God of the Underworld is typically shown with spotted feline ears, a central pointed fang, spiral eyes, and a thin line that forms beneath the squared eyes and twists to form a "cruller" on the bridge of the nose or the brow.[62] Deity GIII from Palenque may be a conflation of the Jaguar God of the Underworld. His shrine is the Temple of the Sun, indicating that GIII was the warrior sun, tied closely to the Underworld.[63] The scene panel of the Temple of the Sun depicts a cave within the Earth—the Underworld into which GIII journeys every night.[64]

## MAYA LUNAR DEITIES

The Maya also recognized a complex of lunar deities, with different genders and ages correlating with particular lunar roles and phases. These lunar deities have been identified as Deity I, Deity O, Lunar Maize God, and Xbalanque, who may also be Deity CH.[65] The female lunar deities are typically associated with water, the Earth, corn, weaving, and divination, motherhood, pregnancy, and childbirth.[66] Many myths and artworks also depict a younger female lunar deity as the wife or partner of the sun deity.[67] Older women in general were commonly associated with transition, power, midwifery, and sometimes danger; they were typically the only women that were allowed to play active roles in the state-sponsored calendrical ceremonies.[68] Male lunar deities have been frequently identified with heroism, sacred essence energy, hunting, corn, the jaguar, and interactions with other planets or celestial alignments.[69]

Many of the Maya lunar deities also had third-gender aspects. Whether these third-gender deities were separate gods altogether, could shapeshift into another gendered aspect of that same deity, or formed a complex under the rubric of one single deity is still unclear, as analyzing these gods outside a presumed binary gender is fairly recent. In the codical images, third-gender lunar deities often signaled a seasonal transition, while more feminized images indicated a likely continuation of the season, good or bad. In other cases, rulers and nobles impersonated the third-gender aspects of Lunar Deity I, who also had aspects of the Maize Deity: netted skirt, jade beads, face markings, and a coiffure.[70] Among ancient Maya elites, it was important to impersonate third-gender deities, because it visually validated their status through costuming, identified them with creator deities, and possibly made them more suitable as both rulers and ritual performers.[71] As mentioned, the sacred attire worn by 18 Rabbit—a netted skirt going below the knee, coupled with a tunic—identified him with a third-gender lunar deity, which legitimized his reign and his role in shamanic imperial ceremonies.[72]

The Popol Vuh indicates that after the Hero Twins defeated the Lords of the Underworld, they became the sun and the moon but does not specify which one of the twins became which. The Título de Totonicapan, a sixteenth-century K'iché' text that parallels the Popol Vuh in many ways, specifies that Xbalanque became the moon, while his brother Hunahpu became the sun.[73] In late Classic ceramic paintings that depict a pair of headband twins, God S may be the Classic counterpart of Hunahpu, while God CH may be Xbalanque. Deity CH is associated with hunting, the jaguar, heroism, and the moon. He is a hero that defeats vain gods.[74] He is depicted with jaguar markings on his body, a ballplayer's belt, and a cruller nose ornament.[75]

Figure 1.1. Lunar deity sitting on a po seat formed by the logograph for the word *moon* in Kekchi, Pokomchi, and Pokoman.

*Drawing 6913 by Linda Schele.*
*Copyright © David Schele.*
*Courtesy of Ancient Americas at LACMA.*

Lunar Deity I has youthful and aged aspects. The younger aspect has been identified as Ixik Kab (Lady Earth in Yucatec Mayan) with Earth, fertility, and lunar aspects.[76] The most important identifying features of young Deity I are the lunar crescent and, in the Classic period, a rabbit and a beak-like appendage projecting out from the upper lip.[77] Lunar Deity I's hair usually contains a curled element in the Kaban day-sign. According to de Landa's alphabet, the Kaban curl corresponds to the phonetic value "u," the Yucatec Mayan term for "moon."[78] During the Postclassic period, Lunar Deity I is identified with a spindle headdress, and her name is frequently accompanied by a *zac* (white) prefix, which may refer to the whiteness of the moon or weaving.[79] She is also sometimes portrayed with a serpent headdress that is shaped as either a figure eight or a lazy eight, which may be glyphic for zac.[80] Young Lunar Deity I is also often depicted as being held by another, which may relate to a specific fertility aspect.

The aged Lunar Deity I is usually depicted with an open jaw and one tooth, a Roman nose, a marking underneath her eyes or on her cheek denoting wrinkles, and sometimes a jutting jaw.[81] Unlike the young Lunar Deity I, who wears a spindle headdress, she is seen actually weaving, which the younger Deity I does not do (see plate 4).[82] Ethnographic evidence from the contemporary Maya also link the moon and weaving and suggest that weaving in codical images correlates with a coming dry season.[83] It is also common for aged Lunar Deity I to be portrayed as a third-gender deity, either initiating a seasonal transition or the warning of one. Third-gender aged Lunar Deity I is typically seen with a woman's long huipil skirt but does not have breasts (see plate 5).

Lunar Deity O, who can be either female or third-gender, is always portrayed as aged. Lunar Deity O is associated with weaving, aspects of the moon and agriculture, fertility, midwifery, divination, medicine, and sweat baths. Along with sharing the aged characteristics of Deity I, Deity O is also often depicted with a red body, and her name usually has a *chac* prefix, signifying "red" or "great," and *chel* ("rainbow" in

Yucatec Mayan).[84] As Chac Chel, she is known as the female half of the original creator couple.[85] Mesoamerican scholar Karl Taube states that the phonetic reading of the deity's name strongly suggests that she is Ix Chel.[86] On the island of Cozumel, there was a talking idol named Ischel (Ix Chjel), where people went to fulfill their vows, make offerings, and ask for help.[87] Diego de Landa states that she is the goddess of childbirth and medicine and describes midwives as her patrons.[88] The Ritual of the Bacabs* records four variants of Ix Chel associated with different colors: red, white, black, and yellow. The variations of Deity O's name may reflect different phases of the moon.[89]

In her feminine form, Lunar Deity O is shown wearing a long huipil skirt. Her breasts or a breast is often visible. She is holding an inverted jug that has water coming out and has a knotted belt possibly representing an umbilical cord and birth rope. The knotted belt could also suggest the fertility of new crops during a continuing rainy season. Thus, instead of a seasonal transition, the feminine-gendered augury indicates that the Earth is in the midst of a rainy season. Lunar Deity O can also have jaguar hands and eagle talons for feet and can wear a long skirt with crossbones, likely recalling previous cataclysmic floods or warning of destructive water (see plate 6).[90] In her third-gender aspect, she can have anthropomorphic aspects, a long woman's skirt, and inverted water jug, but she has no breasts.

*The Ritual of the Bacabs is an eighteenth-century Yucatec Maya manuscript on curanderismo consisting of forty-two principal incantations with fragmentary supplements. The text reflects ancient Maya beliefs along with Christian interpolations. León-Portilla et al., *Language of Kings,* 398; Buenaflor, *Cleansing Rites of Curanderismo,* 60.

# 3

# Dawn, Sunrise, and Morning

## *Rites of Creation and Coming into Being*

Dawn, sunrise, and morning are ideal periods to create, open new pathways, set new beginnings into motion, and conduct divination and manifestation work. Dawn is when light begins to appear in the sky, but before the top of the sun reaches the horizon and becomes visible. Sunrise is when the leading edge of the sun becomes visible and rises above the horizon; this lasts about five minutes. Morning is when the sun is above the horizon and prior to high noon when the sun has reached its zenith.

The ancient Mexica and Maya associated these periods with creation, reverence, youth, birth, an Upperworld floral paradise, rebirth, resurrection, change, accession, the discipline of devotion, conflict, purification, and coming into being. There was reverence and celebration for the fact that the sun had succeeded in making its way out of the Underworld and would once again illuminate the Earth and its inhabitants with sacred essence energy.

Dawn was generally understood as a time of creation, when the sun, maize, and life itself were created. Sunrise was a period of divination and manifestation, and a time when sacred tools, such as medicine bundles, were created and infused with the sun's sacred energy. Morning was when the people revitalized their bodies with the first meal of the day, and shamans would perform limpias for physical spaces and the sacred items within them. People regardless of class, age, or sex engaged in daily offerings to the morning sun and in rituals that reflected the energies of this period.

## DAWN

*Rebirth and Revitalization*

For both the Mexica and the Maya, dawn was generally understood as the time of creation of the sun and the world, and of corn and life itself.[1] It marked a time of nascence, rebirth, and resurrection. The young sun deity made its daily resurrection out of the Underworld and rose with the souls of royal ancestors, brave warriors, gods, and other supernatural beings to travel through an Upperworld floral paradise, the sun's path during the day.[2] This floral paradise, or Flower World, was a place where the souls of the brave and fortunate would spend eternity in happiness and bliss.[3] While some mythological variations existed, it was generally believed that brave warriors and royal ancestors would begin their journey with the resurrected sun at dawn. Along with the feathered serpent, they would sweep the way for the sun, ensuring that it would reach its daily zenith.[4]

In architecture, Flower World was portrayed as a pyramid with stairways, often flanked with plumed serpents and flower symbols serving as a floral road and a conduit for supernatural beings.[5] Flower World was ubiquitous in ancient Mesoamerican art as a paradisal dwelling place for ancestors, as well as the means by which ancestors and gods ascended into the sky.[6] The sarcophagus lid of ruler K'inich Janaab' Pakal I in Classic Palenque, for example, depicts his departure out of the Underworld and his resurrection along a World Tree, which acts as an axis mundi or portal that transfers his body to the Flower World.[7] Pakal wears the symbols of the sun god. Like the sun, he will be reborn into the Flower World at dawn.

Dawn was a period of stability, order, and human existence.[8] At this time, trumpets sounded throughout the Aztec empire, informing the people that it was time to engage in ceremonial offerings, particularly of copal.[9] People engaged in diligent daily offerings to honor the sun and used the dawning sun's energies to enlist divine aid and procure favorable outcomes. These offerings commemorated the sun's defeat of the forces of the Underworld and its resurrection. Drums and conchs from the temples were played, informing shamans and followers that it was time for their dawn rituals.[10]

Temple caretakers would make daily offerings of copal to the sun, images of the gods, and the temples themselves, which were infused with the deity's sacred essence energy. Devotees would go before the images, place copal in ladles, and raise them to honor the spirits of the four directions. They also placed copal in the brazier that stood at the middle of their plazas, which was often seen as the place where the deity resided and was the heart of the temple.[11] Although Sahagún does not provide the specifics, he also mentions that at night people dissolved a black ritual pigment and anointed themselves with it at dawn.[12] They also made offerings of flowers to their deities on their feast days. On the first day of Tlaxochimaco, for example, they held a feast for Huitzilopochtli and decked him and other deities with flowers, garlands, and strings and wreaths of flowers.[13]

Waking up at dawn to make offerings also instilled values and mores, including devotion, humility, and discipline. Mothers and fathers of the Aztec empire woke their children at dawn so they could begin to make their offerings of copal and request divine aid.[14] Noble daughters were instructed to wake up at dawn and make offerings to their deities in the form of passionate spoken invocations, so these deities could make themselves known to the daughters.[15] Fathers told their noble sons to emulate the actions of the *tecutlato* (one holding rank and attributes of a judge) and the *tlacatecutli* (an assisting dignitary to the supreme ruler whose duties were related to military affairs) and at the break of dawn, seize the broom, and sweep.[16]

The ancient Maya also identified dawn with the creation of cycles of time. According to Karl Taube, Classic Maya texts and scenes illustrating the mythical event of the creation of the previous *bak'tun* cycle on 13.0.0.0.0 4 Ajaw 8 Cumk'u (corresponding to August 11, 3114 BCE and ending on December 21, 2012 CE) depict the formation of a three-stone hearth, which also related to the creation of light at the first dawning. The hearth sign is covered as three piled up rocks, prefixed by the sign *yax*, which means "first" or "green" in Yucatec Mayan and is the color for the world center.[17]

In many of the colonial Maya creation mythologies and the invocations of the Ritual of the Bacabs, dawn was analogous to creating life and creation. Throughout the Popol Vuh, it is equated with the creation of life. In the K'iché' Mayan language, to give birth is "to dawn" or "to give light" (*ya' saq*). In Chichicastenango, children are called *alaj q'ij* (little sun) or *alaj q'ij saj* (little ray of sun) when they are mentioned in ritual contexts.[18] The Popol Vuh states:

> There is the sowing of seeds in the earth, whose sprouting will be their dawning. Then there is the matter of human beings, whose sowing in the womb will be followed by their emergence into the light at birth, and whose sowing in the earth at death will be followed by dawning when their souls become sparks of light in the darkness.[19]

The creation myth in the Chilam Balam of Chumayel states, "They [the first gods] moved among the four lights: among the four layers of the stars. The world was not lighted; there was neither day nor night nor moon. Then they perceived that the world was being created. Then creation dawned upon the world. . . . Then a new world dawned for them."[20] The Ritual of the Bacabs also conceives of creation as a cosmic hierogamy that took place at dawn.[21]

Dawn was also an ideal time to locate highly prized stones such as jade, because this is when they were inhaling sacred essence energy from the dawn sun and exhaling their own sacred essence energy as vapor.[22] The Mexica faced the sun and looked for vapor that looked like little smoke strands being emitted from the jade. If they did not immediately find it at the place that was giving off the vapor, they began to dig until they did.[23]

A very dense silicate, jadeite strongly absorbs solar heat. Left in the tropical sun, a polished piece of jade is both burning to the touch and fully capable of producing vapor if moistened.[24] Taube points out that for the ancient Maya, jade was a "rarefied embodiment of life essence, not only as maize and life-giving water, but also as a physical manifestation of the breath spirit"; as an immaterial breath essence of the soul, it allowed for ritual contact with deities and ancestors.[25] According to Sahagún, jade was believed to attract moisture and morning dew and emitted light and rays of sunlight.[26] These qualities, along with its brilliant beauty and the fact that it was one of the hardest and most durable materials in ancient Mesoamerica, no doubt elevated its grandeur.

Ruiz de Alarcón reported that Mesoamerican peoples continued to make offerings to the sun at dawn a hundred years after the Spanish conquest.[27] This rite is still being practiced in the Yucatán. My two principal male mentors, Don Tomas and Don Fernando, who were Yucatec Maya, taught me the importance of this practice and shared their traditions with me. The shamans and other people we work with when my husband and I stay at our villa in Izamal, Yucatán, also have traditions of honoring the sun at dawn and at other times and days. Vicki, our caretaker, who is amazing and multitalented, always shares Maya solar and lunar healing traditions and practices with me as we cook together and prepare the meals for the shamanic retreats my husband and I facilitate at our villa. Marta, one of the persons who cares for our gardens at the Villa, is also a curandera and has taught me her Maya solar limpia traditions. Solar shamanic rites continue to be an integral part of the lives of Maya peoples.

## SUNRISE

*Manifestation and Movement*

For the ancient Mesoamericans, sunrise was a period of coming into being, divination, manifestation, and movement. In the Florentine Codex creation story, once Nanahuatzin threw himself into the pyre, he arose in the sky from the east as the sun. Sahagún writes, "When the sun came to rise, when he burst forth, he appeared to be red. It was impossible to look into his face; he blinded one with his light. Intensely did he shine."[28] This description indicates that this took place at sunrise, when the sun had risen above the horizon.

After the sun and moon rose in the sky, the gods who had gathered at Teotihuacan became gravely concerned because the sun could not move once it was above the horizon. To help it do so, the gods offered themselves to the fire. According to one version of the creation story, sacred medicine bundles were made from the gods' remains.[29] The sun, however, was still unable to move. Ehecatl-Quetzalcoatl then began to blow to help it along.[30]

A Mexica bathing rite in which a midwife identified a baby's name, fortune, and trade was performed at sunrise.[31] Prior to this, a *teteonalmacani* (diviner and shaman) would perform divination to determine the most favorable day to carry it out, based on what the sacred books indicated about the day and time the baby had been born.[32] On the day of the rite, the participants, including the family and many shamans (depending on how many the families could afford), assembled at predawn. When the sun rose, the *tlamatqui* (midwife) began the bathing rite.[33] She would invoke and connect the baby to the divine guidance of its ancestors, breathe into the water, place it in the baby's mouth, and touch the baby's chest and head with it. She then determined the baby's name and fate in life.[34]

## MORNING

*Growth, Cleansing, and Healing*

Morning was a time when the sun was growing in its power and strength. The Mexica often used this period to strengthen their bodies by eating their first meal of the day. They also fed the sacred essence energies of physical spaces and performed limpias for these spaces and the items within them in order to cleanse and renew their energy.[35] On the first day of the month called Toxcatl, early in the morning, shamans from the various precincts went from home to home with incense burners in their hands to give every home a *sahumerio* (smoking) limpia. They would offer incense to cleanse and renew the home, its hearth, and the items in it, including the grinding stone, the tortilla griddle, the pots, small vessels, jugs, plates, bowls, weaving instruments, agricultural implements, storage bins, and artisans' tools.[36]

# RECOMMENDED RITES

### Dawn, Sunrise, and Morning

## WORKING WITH THE ENERGIES OF DAWN

Because creation and rejuvenation energies are ripe at dawn, this is the ideal time for mantras, meditations, trance journeys, limpias, and any other work for creating or recreating.

To access the sacred essence energies of dawn you can, of course, go beyond the recommended rites and create your own rites and infuse the meanings, tools, activities, and regalia associated with dawn. Here is a list of sacred items, meanings, and activities, as well as a sun deity associated with dawn:

- Creation
- Rebirth
- Opening pathways
- Rejuvenation
- Jade
- Flowers
- Offerings to enlist divine assistance
- Breathwork
- Poetry and spoken word
- Eagle paraphernalia
- Solar deity, Xochipilli*

## CONNECTING WITH THE SUN

Before engaging in any of the recommended rites, take a moment to go outside and connect with the sun. Dawn is the safest time to look at the sun's rising light. It is safe to gaze at the sun a few seconds at a time for the first twenty minutes after sunrise and for the last twenty minutes before sunset. Sun gazing at these times is said to have amazing health benefits, including an increased production of melatonin and serotonin (feel-good hormones) and stimulation of the pineal gland, which is largely responsible for our intuition. Gazing at the sun outside these periods can damage the retinas; at these times, please connect with the sun in your mind's eye (close your eyes and visualize it). If you feel called to engage in sun gazing apart from those twenty-minute windows, please be safe and do so in small increments at a time.

You can also close your eyes and envision the sun and connect with whatever phase you are choosing to work with—whether it is the dawn, sunrise, or noon—even at other times of the day. Go beyond visualizing and create a deeper connection by sending a frequency of love to

*See page 31 for more on Xochipilli.

the sun. This process is not so much about working in a time-space paradigm and being precise about the time of day; rather, it is about setting the intention of connecting with the solar energies associated with the particular periods. Nevertheless, doing the rites at the correlating period does strengthen the connection with the sun and links the physical body to the solar processes of that time.

## DAWN MANTRAS

Mantras can be said out loud or silently. Either way, words contain life force energy. In creating your mantra, keep in mind that you are rewiring yourself—that is, strengthening your neural connections with positive thoughts and feelings. If turning your attention to positive thoughts early in the morning is not something you customarily do, you may at first feel that you are forcing yourself to do so. After repeated activity, saying and feeling positive things in the morning will become seamless—self-directed neuroplasticity at work.

Write down your mantra when you have some time to reflect on what you want in your life. Keep it simple enough so you can memorize it quickly and say it repeatedly. Let yourself feel the energy of what you are saying or asking for. Keeping a diamond-sharp focus, state your mantra in the affirmative, preferably in the present tense (as if it is already happening), and include a statement of gratitude: gratitude is a potent manifestation frequency. Stay away from vague statements such as, "I would like" or "I believe." Refrain also from focusing on what you do *not* want: this will only attract more of the same.

Examples of dawn mantra examples could be:

- I am revitalized with the energies of the sun and am grateful for [state what you choose].
- I am one with the sun and am grateful for a life full of [state what you choose].
- I am reborn as of today and am grateful for [state what you choose].

## *Rejuvenation Meditation and Shamanic Breathwork*

Since dawn is the time the young sun exhales his first breath of sacred essence energy, going outside to join the sun at dawn, or envisioning it at dawn, while becoming aware of your breath, will help deepen your meditation. Close your eyes, and inhale and exhale slowly.

Take a moment to connect with the dawn sun. Thank him for rejuvenating you with his youthful sacred essence energies. Continue to focus and become aware of your breath, allowing your heart to remain open to these energies. Through your breath, inhale the dawn energies and let them rejuvenate you on cellular and soul levels. To help absorb this energy and deepen the meditation, engage in the following breathwork exercise:

Sit down with your back straight. Allow the hands to rest easily on the lap with the palms facing up, closing off the electromagnetic circuits from receiving external information and energy and enhancing feelings of centeredness. Inhale, hold your breath, and tighten all of your muscles from your abdomen to your tailbone. Hold the breath for about 30 seconds. Then exhale deeply out of the mouth, release the tightening, and send the energies from your tailbone up your spine, neck, and head to the crown chakra (located slightly above the top of the head). Pause for 30 seconds, and visualize the rays of the dawning sun entering your crown chakra. Repeat this exercise for at least 5 minutes. When you feel complete, thank the sun for rejuvenating you with his sacred essence energies.

## *Drawing in the Sun's Dawn Energy*

Set the intention of drawing in the energies of the sun at dawn. If you want to elaborate on your intention, please feel free to do so. Take a deep inhale while slowly extending the arms out, coming up to the sides of the body. Have the hands meet above the head, let them draw in the sun's dawn energy, and place them in prayer position. Hold the breath for a few seconds, and then bring the hands slowly down in prayer position while exhaling into the heart chakra at the center of the chest. Allow the dawn energy to come into your essence through your hands and heart chakra. Repeat this exercise for at least 5 minutes.

## MORE ELABORATE DAWN RITES

### *Stability and Revitalize with the Sun at Dawn and Orange Juice*

Oranges enhance any magical intention. For this rite, you will need a glass of orange juice. Go outside to where you can offer some orange juice to the Earth. Begin by drawing in the sun's energy with the breathwork exercise. Afterward hold the orange juice in your hands, and thank the sun for charging it with his energies of stability and revitalization. Then take a few drinks of the orange juice. Pour out the rest of the orange juice on the Earth in a circle, with you in the middle. Sit in the middle of the circle, and take a few minutes to connect with the sun at dawn, while focusing on your intention.

### *Opening Pathways with a Fire Limpia*

What you will need for this rite:

- Glazed brazier
- Charcoal tablet
- Wooden matches
- Copal or herbs and flowers (they must be dry) that are wonderful at opening pathways, such as chamomile, lantana, hibiscus, echinacea, basil, and geranium

New fires facilitate and initiate new cycles and can open up pathways. Create a new fire in a firepit or on a charcoal tablet (remember to use a glazed brazier or steel urn if you are using charcoal tablets). Connect with the fire, and thank it for igniting and fueling your intention. Thank your offerings for also helping you with your intention. After you have made your offerings, call upon the sun, and envision and thank the rays of the dawn sun for opening pathways for you. Breathe into your intention and continue to connect with the dawn sun from your sacred heart. When you feel complete, know that this has been done, and thank the sun, fire, and your offerings once again.

## *Creativity and New Beginnings with Red Roses*

For this rite you will need:

- Twelve red roses
- A vase to place the roses in
- Parchment paper
- Water
- A No. 2 pencil

Start by turning your attention to your breath. Inhale and exhale slowly. Let the twelve red roses sit beside you or on your lap as you connect with the sun at dawn.

To go into a trance, you can use one of the recommended shamanic breathwork exercises or repetitive drumbeats. As I explain in *Curanderismo Soul Retrieval,* rhythmic repetitive auditory stimulation with a drum, rattle, or Tibetan bowls affects electrical activity in many sensory and motor areas of the brain. Repetitive auditory rhythms can cause changes in the central nervous system and stimulate visual images of color, pattern, and movement—ideal for trance states. Deep repetitive beats of lower frequencies transmit impulses along neural pathways and induce trance states and link the human heart with the heartbeat of the Earth. The beats should be strong, monotonous, unvarying, and rapid. There should be no contrast in intensity or in the intervals between them.[37]

Once you are in a meditative state, place a soft focus on your intention. Once you are clear about it, write down your petition on a parchment paper with a No. 2 pencil. Place the paper, with the vase of roses on top of it, on your altar or in a special place. Thank the roses daily for helping you. Once they have dried, place them back into the Earth. Leave the paper on your altar. Once your intention comes to be, bury the paper in the Earth.

## *Revitalizing Your Energy Fields with Jade*

For this rite you will need:

- A piece of jade or jadeite
- A bowl (of any size as long as the jade can fit into it)
- Spring or filtered water
- Parchment paper
- A No. 2 pencil

To revitalize your energy fields, remember, everything is energy, and we too have energy bands that extend out from the body, which are called auric energy fields or subtle bodies. These fields are simply reflections of things going on in the physical body and its energy system, while at the same time they affect the body and energy system. They act like antennae, receiving and sending information and transforming this information so it can be used by the body. Stress, trauma, poor health habits, and pollution can cause holes, leaks, and tears in auric fields, which then can cause lethargy, anxiety, depression, susceptibility to other people's emotions, and other ailments.

Every now and then it is a good idea to repair and strengthen our energy fields. This rite is an ideal way to do so.

Allow yourself to go into a trance or meditative state, and then focus on your intention. Once you are clear about your petition, write it down on the paper with the pencil. If you want your energy fields to be revitalized, mention this in your petition; for example, "Thank you, my dawning sun, for filling this piece of jade with your rays of light to revitalize me and strengthen and repair my energy fields."

Place the jade in a bowl of filtered or spring water. Then place the bowl on top of your petition. Leave the bowl of water outside or on a windowsill during dawn. Remove the jade from the water, and bathe with this water in the shower or in a bath. Thereafter, carry the piece of jade with you, preferably on your skin or in a pocket, and thank it for repairing and strengthening your energy fields that day. Depending on the level of stress or toxicity you have been exposed to, you may need to do this practice repeatedly.

## WORKING WITH THE ENERGIES OF SUNRISE

For the ancient Maya and Mexica, sunrise marked the movement of a sun that could sustain and nourish this world. This was a time for manifestation, divination, bringing something into being, awareness, connecting with ancestors for guidance and aid, and movement. The following is a list of sacred items and rituals, as well as a sun deity associated with sunrise:

- Divination
- Manifestation rites
- Taking action
- Water limpias
- Sweeping limpias
- Flowers
- Breathwork
- Making medicine bundles, or charging the sacred items that are in the medicine bundle
- Solar deity, Tonatiuh*

### *Motivation and Movement for Your Day*

The energies of sunrise can be incredibly inspirational for taking action. They are ideal for creating and prioritizing your path for the day.

Go outside to greet the sun emerging out of the horizon. If you miss this event, close your eyes and envision a sunrise. Thank the sun for infusing you with the wisdom, discipline, and sacred essence energy to plan your day and take action with impeccability.

Take a few minutes to engage in some centering shamanic breathwork. This helps to induce a trance meditative state. As you are connecting with the sunrise, either with your eyes open or closed, inhale for 12 seconds with your tongue touching the roof of your mouth. Hold the breath for

*See pages 29–30 for more on Tonatiuh.

12 seconds, and exhale slowly for another 12 seconds with your tongue touching the bottom of your front teeth; the tongue is slightly outside the mouth. If you cannot do 12 seconds, try starting with 6 seconds and work your way up to 12.

Now take at least 5 more minutes to envision your day, or better yet, create a simple to-do list on your phone or computer. Remember, prioritizing and organizing your day in a relaxed, inspired state is disciplined self-care. We know what we can and cannot do, and what we may ultimately have to delegate to another day or to someone else. Taking action through balanced inspiration rather than blindly also helps to reduce stress in our lives.

### ◎ *Divination for the Day*

Sunrise is an ideal time to do divination. Let the sunrise inspire or charge your course of action. Again, if you can go outside to connect with the sun as it rises, that would be perfect. If not, then just visualize it. Either way, connect to the sunrise, and thank the sun for guiding your course of action. Take slow, mindful breaths in and out of the nose.

After you have connected with the sunrise, engage in your preferred divination work, such as picking a card from your favorite Tarot deck. If you do not care for the answer or are not clear about it, connect with the sunrise again and ask for alternatives or clarification. If you like the answer, place the card next to a picture of you on your altar or some other special place, and let the sunrise and the intention of the card direct and create your day.

## MORE ELABORATE SUNRISE RITES

### ◎ *Creating a Manifestation Medicine Bundle*

For this rite you will need:

- Honey
- Flowers (dry or fresh) that strengthen intentions, such as echinacea, hibiscus, or orange flowers
- Parchment paper

- A No. 2 pencil
- Cloth, preferably of a single color—blue is used for serenity and tranquility; red attracts love, health, and power; pink is for good will; green removes harmful or negative influences; purple repels dense energies; black absorbs; and white purifies
- Cinnamon powder for enhancing the intention

Just as sacred medicine bundles were made at sunrise in the creation story of the sun, my mentors taught me to create medicine bundles and charge them with sunrise energies. This always includes offering prayers to the bundle to revitalize its life force.

Medicine bundles are multifaceted in purpose and meaning, which can encompass healing, manifestation, cleansing, and revitalization. The bundle itself can be a plain or beautifully embroidered cloth or an animal skin and can contain various sacred items. One bundle on my altar contains corn for divination; special crystals—amber, amethyst, and lapis lazuli; divination cards; and tobacco. I work with this medicine bundle to heal and work with the earth's ley-line systems.

Start by connecting with the energies of sunrise, and send a frequency of love to the sun at sunrise. Then write down your intention on the paper.

Place a little bit of honey on the parchment paper and a few flowers on top of the honey. Then sprinkle some cinnamon on the paper. Fold the paper twice into a square, and place it on the cloth. Place more flowers on the cloth, and tie it with a piece of cloth, making a small medicine bundle. Tie it 3 times, each time blowing into the tie, and state your intention each time. Place the bundle in your purse or pocket, and keep it on you until your intention comes to pass. Then bury the bundle in the earth, or leave it on your altar or somewhere that is special for you.

## *Baños with Flowers for Inspiration and Happiness*

As I explain in *Cleansing Rites of Curanderismo,* water limpias (*baños*) were one of the most prevalent and revered cleansing rites among the ancient Mesoamerican shamans. Bathing in water, being cleansed by water, and entering water fostered pivotal life transitions, including birth, adolescence, accession of shaman rulers, death, renewal, and resurrection. Taking a baño at sunrise or while connecting to sunrise imprints the intention of the baño onto our auric fields, which is particularly helpful if we need to strengthen them for that day and move any energetic blocks or stagnant energies. Remember, baños also cleanse and revitalize the mind, body, and spirit.

For this baño, you will need:

- A bathtub or a small kid-sized pool
- A cup of Epsom salts
- A bundle of any dry herbs (all herbs have cleansing properties) to cleanse your space
- A handful (your hand) of fresh flowers, or half a handful of dry flowers

You can use a combination of flowers, depending on what you feel you need.

Most flowers invite good fortune and happiness, and here are some of their other gifts:

**Calendula (marigold)** clears energetic toxins stemming from thoughts and feelings. Greatly enhances happiness and health and alleviates depression. Accelerates any healing process.

**Chamomile** reverses misfortunes to great fortune. Promotes peace, harmony, prosperity, and positivity. Enhances, soothes, and balances energy fields.

**Daisy** has divinatory qualities concerning love. Increases self-awareness, creativity, and inner strength. Helps to get stagnant energies and situations moving.

**Lavender** clears monkey chatter, stress, confusion, and disharmony. Helps to be in divine alignment in all areas of our life. Reminds us of our true divine Self and clears pathways within our lives and energy fields so we can realize equanimity. Attracts sensuous and playful love. Enhances the energy field, and helps to gracefully release guilt and shame.

**Rose** is a very powerful source of purification. Helps to strengthen energy fields and enhance self-love. Calms tense energies, and attracts love.

Start by cleaning and cleansing the location. One simple way is to smudge it with a bundle of dry herbs. Communicate with the spirit essence of the herbs or flowers before using them, and thank them for helping to purify and rejuvenate you. Place them in a clean twelve-cup coffee or tea maker to make concentrated tea. A handful of dry herbs or flowers (squeeze in twice as many if the herbs or flowers are fresh) should yield five to seven pots; you can tell you have extracted what you want from them when the water becomes very light. Place the cup of Epsom salts and the concentrated tea in the tub or pool.

Once you are in the tub or pool, connect with the sun at sunrise, spirit essence of the water and flowers, and thank them for cleansing and rejuvenating you and for bringing more inspiration and happiness in your life. While in the water, strengthen your intention by calmly focusing on it and being grateful for it. When you feel you are complete with the baño, exit the tub and thank the sun, water, and the spirit of the flowers one last time. Afterward, wash off with cold water, which clears away any residual unwanted energies. Hot- and cold-water hydrotherapy also benefits the body, boosting circulation, reducing stress, and removing toxins from the organs.

## WORKING WITH THE ENERGIES OF MORNING

For the ancient Maya and Mexica, the sun at morning was rising and continuing to grow and mature. Morning is an ideal time to create, manifest, do divination work, engage in limpias, and strengthen our energy fields. The ancient Mesoamerican midwives continued their divination work at the bathing rites of babies from sunrise through the morning. Any work done in the morning can grow and expand by simply connecting with the morning sun.

Recommended rites and activities for the morning encompass the sunrise rites, especially since sunrise proper lasts about five minutes and continues into early morning. If you create a mantra to connect with the energies of the morning sun, continue to repeat it throughout the morning, while intermittently connecting with the sun and letting it charge you and your intentions.

### ◎ *Cleansing Yourself with Cobra Pranayama Breathwork*

Connect with the morning sun, and thank him for cleansing you. Then position your hands according to the cobra acupressure points: Cup your hands over your face. Place the index fingers on the temples and place pressure there. The index, middle, and ring fingers should be slightly above the eyebrows. Place the pinkies at the bridge of the nose, and put pressure there.

These acupressure points also relieve most kinds of headaches and help us to become more focused, centered, and grounded.

Keep your hands in the cobra position, and take quick breaths in from the abdomen, while pushing in or contracting the abdomen. Bring the breath to your chest. Count to either 11, 22, or 33 while doing the Cobra Pranayama breathing. After you count to 11, 22, or 33, exhale out the mouth (refrain from exhaling while engaging in the quick inhales). Repeat this breathing exercise three times with the same set of counting to 11, 22, or 33; counting to these master numbers helps to induce a slight trance state.

### ◎ *Inspiration and Happiness Teas Made of Flowers*

You can use fresh flowers or dry flowers for these teas. Generally you will need twice as many fresh flowers as dry ones, approximately 1.5 to 2 teaspoons of dried flowers and 2 to 4 teaspoons of fresh flowers for 8 ounces of tea. Refer to the flowers identified for baños in the section on pages 56–58 to determine what kind of flower tea you will make. Steep the tea for 5 to 6 minutes.

If you would like more inspiration and happiness in your life, take the tea 3 or 4 times a day for a period of 7 days. Remember to connect with the spirit essence of the morning sun, water, and flowers before drinking it.

## MORE ELABORATE MORNING RITES

### *Cleansing a Space with Sahumerio Limpias*

A sahumerio cleanses a living space by filling it with sacred smoke from a prepared mixture or resins. You will need the following for a sahumerio:

- Charcoal tablets (get larger tablets)
- A steel or glazed brazier
- Wooden matches
- Copal

Connect with the morning sun, and thank it for strengthening your intention to cleanse and revitalize the sacred essence energy of your living space. Start by opening the doors of the house, or your room if you are just cleansing your room. Temporarily turn off the smoke alarms. Opening up the windows is helpful, but it is the doors that must be kept open, because they are the main gateway through which energies enter and leave. Light the charcoal in the brazier, and place the copal on it. For every room, begin by smoking out the four corners, and then continue to clear it out by moving your hand that is holding the brazier in a clockwise spiral direction. This motion is said to encircle and clear out any types of dense energies. Sing a song as an additional offering for the limpia.

Once you are done, connect with the morning sun again, and thank it again for joining you in cleansing and feeding the sacred essence energy of your room.

---

**Michael Retrieves Soul Pieces**

As I explain in my book *Curanderismo Soul Retrieval*, working with the sun and engaging in breathwork are excellent ways to bring back pieces of the soul that have left because of traumas. I focus on creating loving, healthy, and honoring spaces within ourselves so the soul pieces are inspired to stay as they come back.

Part of creating such spaces is to engage in daily rites of self-love. Drawing in the sun's dawn energy is an ideal way to replenish ourselves with the sun's sacred essence energy, so we in turn have enough energy to move forward on the path of self-love. Rejuvenating ourselves with a pure source of sacred essence energy such as the sun is particularly helpful if we feel drained, depressed, or confused. This simple exercise is one rite I recommend to my clients when they need an immediate boost of pure sacred essence energy.

When Michael first came to me, he was not taking care of himself, letting his practice as a therapist unravel, and having a difficult time caring for his son during his turns of partial custody. He was referred to me by one of my prior clients, who worked in the same building with him as a therapist. When she first came to me, she had been at a similar, though perhaps less severe, low, so she strongly advised him to come and see me.

It took him more than a month to finally commit to his first session. When he finally came to see me, he told me that his fiancée of four years had left him because of his unwillingness to change. He experienced constant mood swings when he was with her, despite the antidepressants and other medications he was taking. He would shut down and be completely reclusive for long periods of time. He loved her deeply nonetheless, and he relied on her to give him the sacred essence energy he needed to keep going. When she left, he fell apart, because he no longer had this source of energy and did not have the tools to obtain his own.

Michael had hardly any motivation to do anything. He was barely eating and told me that he already lost more than ten pounds in the last two weeks (although I suspect it was a little more than ten pounds). He was constantly canceling many of his appointments with his clients and was significantly behind on the client notes that he had to submit for his clinic. He had already received his first verbal warning. When he had his son, he was unable to cook or care for him the way he normally did. Instead he mainly served fast-food meals.

Fortunately, his son was fairly responsible, so he did his homework and other chores on his own.

I knew that Michael needed an immediate source of pure sacred essence energy, so in our first session, I took him on a journey to the sun at dawn to rejuvenate him. After our platica, followed by the Cobra Pranayama breathing and a Florida water limpia, I journeyed with him and took his I Am presence to the dawn sun. I requested that the dawn sun provide his I Am presence a continuous infusion of sacred essence energy, especially when he called on it. Although he felt substantially better after our session, I told him that in order to maintain this elevated frequency, he had to do his own work outside of our sessions. I taught him how to draw in the dawn sun's energy. I needed to recommend a rite that would be practical enough for him to do but strong enough for him to feel the effects.

In our next session two weeks later, I could tell he was finally eating, he had caught up with his client notes, and he was beginning to enjoy his time with his son again. He was also smiling and laughing: a dramatic shift. Most importantly, every day he was drawing in the dawn sun's sacred essence energy, and he noticed that he was more motivated to take care of his responsibilities after engaging in this rite. He shared with me his lack of self-love and self-esteem, particularly about where he was at in his career and his lack of motivation to do anything about it. Once again, we journeyed to the dawn sun to replenish him with motivation and zest for life. I recommended that he continue to draw in the dawn sun's energy, now focusing on allowing himself to feel this rejuvenation.

In our second session a month later, he told me that he had applied to four universities to obtain his doctorate. He was eating regularly and feeling substantially better about himself. He was also going back to the gym, had joined us at one of our breathwork classes, and was integrating breathwork practices to continue to move forward on his path of self-love.

Although we still had many other childhood and relationship issues that we needed to work on with soul-retrieval practices, I share this story to point out that drawing in the sun's energy is a practical and effective way to rejuvenate us on the levels of mind, body, and spirit.

---

# 4

# High Noon and Afternoon

## *Rites of Power, Leadership, and Release*

For the ancient Mesoamericans, high noon, when the sun is at its highest altitude or zenith, was when the sun was at its strongest and gave its greatest degree of sacred essence energy. Deceased valiant warriors, virtuous nobles, and rulers were believed to carry the sun from dawn to its daily zenith at high noon, so this period was equated with courage, greatness, and honor. The sun at the zenith, at its height in power and strength, also initiated the beginning of the day according to the Mexica and some Maya solar calendars.[1]

Afternoon, approximately about an hour past high noon until sunset, marked Nepantla-Tonatiuh, a liminal period when the sun was declining in power, strength, and virility. As the sun declined, it was seen as maturing and becoming old. This older sun was escorted from its zenith to sunset by brave warrior women who died in childbirth, the Cihuateteo.[2] During the afternoon, the aging sun was comforted and honored with incense, ritual dancing, and singing. This time of the day was also identified with spiritual wisdom, increased soul-essence energy, and at times, some dangerous aspects of old age, reflected in *brujas* (witches) who were skilled in magic and in cloaking their motives.

## HIGH NOON

*Power, Strength, Leadership, and Revitalization*

The Mexica associated the sun at high noon with peak strength, courage, honor, and leadership. They identified themselves as "the people of the sun." Their beloved tutelary war deity, Huitzilopochtli, personified the sun at its height, at high noon.[3] At the start of Huitzilopochtli's sign under the tonalpohualli calendar, ce tecpatl (1 Flint), they cleansed his sacred ornaments and placed them in the sun at this time of the day to revitalize and charge them with sacred essence energy.[4] The Sun Stone represented the sun at its zenith, in its full glory.[5] As discussed in chapter 1, the image in the middle of the Sun Stone also likely personified the solar deities Tonatiuh and Huitzilopochtli and the rulers Moctezuma I and II. These figures, who were believed to exemplify courage, strength, and valor, were associated with the sun at high noon.

High noon may have also been identified with the birth of a new day. Few Spanish ethnographers of the sixteenth century considered the possibility of different times for the beginning of a day in distinct indigenous day-counting systems. Nonetheless, the commentator on folio 48 of the Codex Telleriano-Remensis states that the Aztecs "count the day from noon to the noon of the next day." Fray Juan de Córdoba also noted that the Zapotecs "counted the day from noon to noon." Consequently, Mesoamerican scholar Alfonso Caso has suggested that in both of the Mexica calendars, the tonalpohualli and the *xiuhpohualli*, days began at noon.[6] Robert Redfield's early twentieth-century ethnographic research into the Chan Kom, a Yucatec Maya village, suggests that they recognized noon as the beginning of a day. He reported that they used noon as the marker for determining the baby's name and fate.[7]

High noon was also the time when most people ate the largest meal of the day, and when many ritual fasts ended. Like the sun at his height in radiating sacred essence energy, the body was maintained at its height in strength by being nourished with the largest meal.[8] The *pipiltzin* (nobles) then had the luxury of recharging their bodies at the hottest time of the day with a siesta until the trumpets and drums sounded, marking the midafternoon.[9]

The principal meal of Mexica state-sponsored alms also took place at high noon. Starting on the first day of the eighth month, Uei Tecuilhuitl, the state fed the poor for eight days. In the morning the state gave them as much *atole,* a corn-based porridge, as they could consume. At high noon, the state replenished the poor by feeding them as many tamales as they could carry. These consisted of fruit, lime-treated corn blossoms, honey, green beans, and grains of corn.[10]

## AFTERNOON

*Decreasing, Aging, and Spiritual Wisdom*

The afternoon marked an important liminal period, which was associated with advanced age and brave warrior women. The sun deity progressively aged as he waned from his peak strength at high noon. By the time he arrived into the Underworld, he was depicted as an old man. In the Underworld sequence of the Codex Borgia on page 35, the sun deity Yohualtecuhtli appears as an elderly man with Tonatiuh's facial markings and wearing a crocodile skin (see plate 7).[11]

In the afternoon, the Mexica sounded trumpets and drums to inform everyone that it was time to make offerings to the sun.[12] Ritual singing and dancing were commonly offered to soothe the sun as it was aging during this liminal period, Nepantla-Tonatiuh. Nepantla was identified as a liminal middle space. It was important to honor the sun in these ambiguous spaces, and of course before his journey into the Underworld.

After the sun reached its zenith, the Cihuateteo, the Mexica women who died in childbirth, carried the sun to sunset.[13] Giving birth was seen as symbolic combat, in which the Cihuateteo were seen as valiant warriors. The midwife gave a woman in labor a toy shield and spears to help her fight her battle.[14] When the baby was born, the midwife gave war cries, which meant that the mother had fought a good battle, had become a brave warrior, and captured a baby.[15] During the sun's journey from high noon to sunset, the Cihuateteo carried the sun on a mantle of quetzal feathers and marched before it, shouting with joy and praising the sun until delivering it to the west at sunset.[16]

The Mexica associated advanced age with increased sacred essence energy, especially for people that had lived for fifty-two years. It was believed that a fifty-two-year-old had been reheated with the interior fire of the sun and consequently had more tonalli. Elders were generally more respected, seen as being wiser, and more in tune with the rhythms of the cosmos.[17] They were also allowed to drink pulque (an alcoholic beverage made from the maguey plant) until inebriated. This privilege was only granted to others mainly during particular sunset and evening rites.[18] When a woman turned fifty, she was respected for her counsel and allowed to make long speeches, and her domestic obligations ended.[19]

The Maya may have viewed elders in general as figures of authority and wisdom; the codices, artwork, and mythologies often depicted elder women as warriors and warrior midwives.[20] Old age may, however, have been more of a perceptual than actual idealization. Few living lords were depicted as elders, and elders were depicted as deities, such as the creator deities of the Popol Vuh, Xmucane and Xpiacoc.[21]

While Maya elders in general may have been viewed as figures of authority and wisdom, elder women were sometimes depicted as dangerous grandmother brujas, such as the one in the Popol Vuh who tried to kill the Hero Twins as babies.[22]

In the Mexica tenth month of Xocotl Uetzi, the Great Feast of the Dead was associated with the collection of the fruits of the Earth and the ritual death of plants, the Underworld, the night, and the dead. In the afternoon of this feast, the people honored the sun with ritual dancing and singing to take him into the Underworld. The men, youths, and small boys assembled in the main plaza, wearing beautiful multicolored feathers. They would sing and dance the serpent dance until it was dark. The women would dance in between the men,[23] possibly simulating the brave Cihuateteo, who marched before the sun and delivered him to sunset.

At the start of the Mexica eleventh month, Ochpaniztli (sweeping of the way), the people swept the streets of the town, the sweat baths, and all the corners of their houses; cleaned all of their possessions; and engaged in five days of silence. On the afternoon of the fifth day, they enacted a hand-waving dance in the afternoon in honor of the grandmother deity Toci.[24] Toci, as mentioned, had lunar aspects and was also associated with aging, white, death, the hummingbird, the house of the sun (probably because of her warrior aspects), and terrestrial goddesses. The people formed into four rows and, holding bunches of flowering marigolds, danced until sunset. They repeated this dance every day from afternoon to sunset for at least three days.[25]

## RECOMMENDED RITES

### High Noon and Afternoon

## WORKING WITH THE ENERGIES OF HIGH NOON

When working with high noon, I recommend going on the internet to look up when the sun is at its highest altitude in your area. An easy site to navigate that is loaded with great information on the positions of the sun and moon in particular areas around the world is timeanddate.com. Working within one hour of the daily zenith of the sun, one hour before or after, will still be potent enough to garner the energies of high noon.

Here are some sacred items, some activities, and a solar deity associated with the energies of high noon:

- Recharging the physical body
- Reenergizing sacred items

- Revitalizing breathwork
- Activities that require a show of strength, courage, and leadership
- Fire rites, especially those coupled with snake totems
- Turquoise stones
- Headdresses with turquoise or hummingbird paraphernalia
- Hummingbird and snakes, and sacred images or items connected with them, such as feathers, snakeskin, and snake fangs or teeth (as long as they are obtained ethically)
- Ritual offerings
- Solar deity, Huitzilopochtli*

## HIGH NOON MANTRAS FOR DIVINE POWER AND PEAK STRENGTH

Connecting to the sacred energies of high noon is perfect for garnering more power, particularly equalizing power dynamics, building authentic self-confidence and self-love, and stimulating strength and vitality.

Before engaging in any mantras, take a moment or two to connect with the sun at high noon. You can go outside and invite the sun's high-noon energy into you, or you can close your eyes and visualize the sun directly above you radiating and nourishing you with his sacred essence energy. Here are some sample mantras for high noon:

- I am the sacred energies of the high-noon sun. I am always in my full divine power.
- I am the sacred energies of the high-noon sun. I am divine self-confidence and love and adore myself.
- I am the sacred energies of the high-noon sun. I emulate divine strength and vitality.

*For more on Huitzilopochtli see pages 30 and 65.

## Journeying to the Flower Realm

This meditative journey and breathwork help to instill feelings of power and strength from a graceful and balanced space, rather than with the typical harshness associated with these qualities.

You can do this trance journey by cleansing and recharging your body with breathwork first, or you can go straight into the journey; it depends on how readily you can go into a trance state and whether you enjoy breathwork. Because it induces calm trance states and replenishes sacred essence energy, I always recommend it.

### Purifying with Breath of Fire

The Breath of Fire exercise can purify and replenish us holistically. Start by sitting with your spine straight in a butterfly pose, with the soles of the feet touching so the legs are in a diamond shape, or cross your legs in a comfortable position, with the feet underneath the opposite knee. If neither of these is an option for you, sit in a chair where your spine can be straight.

Quickly breathe in and out of the nose. Pull the abdomen in toward the diaphragm during the exhalation and out during inhalation. (If you are unfamiliar with Breath of Fire, watch a YouTube video that shows how to do it.) Continue Breath of Fire for 30 seconds to a minute, or longer, and intertwine it with the following facial mudra.*

### Raising Adrenaline with a Facial Mudra

This facial mudra raises a balanced flow of adrenaline, which can inspire graceful feelings of power and strength. Start by taking a deep inhale, and extend your tongue out toward your chin while engaging in a nasal exhale. Repeat sticking your tongue out with nasal exhales 3 times. Then go back to Breath of Fire, and repeat the deep inhales and exhales with your tongue

*Mudras are postures that trigger and speed up electromagnetic charges in the body. Like acupressure points, they stimulate particular areas of the body and correlating energetic systems. There are different kinds of mudras, involving the body, face, and hands.

out. Repeat the cycle one last time, so you have done the Breath of Fire and tongue out exhales for three complete cycles.

This mudra—with tongue down to the chin—is identified with power and strength in different traditions. Huitzilopochtli and Tonatiuh, displayed at the center of the Sun Stone, and the Hindu goddess Kali, destroyer of illusions, are shown with this mudra.

### Balancing Breathwork

Finally, inhale through the nose for a full 6 seconds. Hold the breath for 6 seconds. Then exhale out of the mouth for a full 6 seconds. Repeat until you feel relaxed in a slight trance state.

### Journey within the Sacred Heart

Set the intention of connecting with the divine presence within you, your I Am presence, and journeying to sun at high noon through your sacred heart—the space where you are infinite, untouchable, pure love. If you are having trouble connecting with your I Am, a powerful and effective method for doing so is both a command and a statement of truth: "Stand aside, ego, in the name of God: I Am That I Am." (I use the term *God* free of any particular religious association, but rather to name a principle of divine love. If you do not feel comfortable with the term *God,* use a word or concept that signifies pure Divinity, Love, and Consciousness to you.)

Visualize a mirror reflection of yourself as your divine I Am presence in front of you. This is the Self that is always encouraging you and inspiring you to be patient, loving, tender, and compassionate with yourself and others. It is the you that is pure love and only love; the real *you.* Now look at your I Am, and allow yourself to fall more deeply in love with *you,* opening your heart to *you* more and more.

Now see your I Am become infinitely small, standing on a zero-point stream of light radiating out from your sacred heart. Walk into and toward the sacred heart as your I Am presence. The first doorway into the sacred heart is the violet fires of transfiguring divine love and infinite physical perfection. Allow the violet fires to completely encompass you, caress you, and love you. Place into them any lower emotions or beliefs that you are ready to let go of, including fears, doubts, and regrets. Allow yourself to remain in the violet fires throughout this journey, releasing energies that you are ready to let go of, as well as things that may come up in the journey. Remember, within the sacred heart you are multidimensional and can be in many places at one time.

The second doorway into the sacred heart is the white fires of purification and resurrection. Allow these white fires also to completely encompass you, caress you, and love you. Let these white fires inspire you and remind you of your infinite potential. As you step into your sacred heart, see yourself in a floral paradise, a place like the Garden of Eden, where everything is alive—the numerous flowers surrounding you and all of nature welcoming you home.

A handsome bronze deity, Huitzilopochtli, welcomes you to this paradisal realm, Xochicalli (the place or house of flowers). He takes you over to a lake of floating *chinampas,* rectangular strips of floating beds of vegetation, where luminous beings are sunbathing. He invites you to get on one of the sunbathing beds. Get on the bed and lie down. As you are lying on the floating bed in the lake, let the high noon replenish you and fill you with divine power, strength, and vitality. Know that the magic of Xochicalli and its chinampas will recalibrate your sacred essence energy to an ideal balance of power and strength.

Once you have had your fill of sacred essence energy from the high noon, exit from Xochicalli through your sacred heart. Visualize yourself in the sacred white fires of purification and resurrection, and then in the violet fires. The sacred fire angels here congratulate you for taking the time to do something loving and nurturing for yourself. Then take six deep inhales and exhales, inhaling into the nose and exhaling out of the mouth. Gently rub your thighs with your hands, coming back fully present and grounded.

## ◉ *Sunbathing with Crystals*

This ceremony helps to cleanse, energize, and clear blocks within our energy centers (chakras) and subtle energetic bodies. Each chakra resonates with a particular frequency and is associated with specific colors, which also vibrate at particular frequencies. You can place the crystal of the corresponding color on the chakra. This will help to clear any blocks in the chakras, ensure they are resonating at an optimum frequency, and provide you with more energy through the energies of the high-noon sun and the crystals.

You can also depart from the color correspondences and place crystals on your chakras according to their gifts and properties, based on what you feel you need energetically.

### Chakras, Colors, and Properties of Crystals

1. **Root chakra and red crystals.** The root chakra is located at the base of the spine, inside the vagina in women and above the testicles in men. Working with the root chakra can help to ground and center us. The color associated with the root chakra is red. Red crystals raise and ground energy.
2. **Sacral chakra and orange crystals.** The sacral chakra is found just below the navel in the center of the body. Working with the sacral chakra can help us to feel emotionally balanced. The color associated with this chakra is orange. Orange crystals can help to move, release, and balance energies.
3. **Solar plexus and yellow crystals.** The solar plexus is between the navel and sternum. Working with this center can enhance personal will and sense of power. The color associated with the solar plexus is yellow. Yellow crystals help to reduce tension and revitalize and balance power.
4. **Heart chakra and green or pink crystals.** The heart chakra is located behind the sternum. Working with the heart chakra can induce peace, compassion, and love. The heart chakra is associated with the colors green and pink. Green crystals promote peace and understanding. Pink crystals induce calmness, softness, and compassion.
5. **Throat chakra and blue crystals.** The throat chakra sits right above the hollow base of the neck. Working with the throat chakra can aid communication and creativity. The throat chakra is associated with

the color blue. Blue crystals bring a sense of balance and intuitive knowing.

6. **Third eye and indigo crystals.** The third eye chakra is at the center of the forehead. Working with the third eye develops imagination, discernment, and intuition. This chakra is typically associated with indigo. Indigo crystals can enhance intuitive gifts.
7. **Crown chakra and violet crystals.** The crown chakra is located above the very top of the head. Working with the crown chakra can develop inspiration and expansiveness. The crown chakra is associated with violet. Violet crystals enhance spiritual growth and awareness.

Go outside to sunbathe for 15 to 20 minutes between 12 p.m. and 3 p.m., and lay crystals along your energy centers to cleanse and energize you. The ancient Mexica ritually sunbathed to garner sacred essence energy, although too much sun was believed to have adverse effects. If possible, do this ceremony after you have taken a baño (see pages 56–58 for instructions). As you are lying down, set the intention of connecting with the energies of the sun at high noon. Thank the high-noon sun for cleansing and energizing you and for whatever additional intentions you have included in your sunbathing rite.

## MORE ELABORATE HIGH NOON RITES

### ◎ *Manifesting with a Water Limpia Rite and the Stamina of the High Noon Sun*

For this rite you will need:

- A clear bowl or glass (do not use this glass or bowl to eat from; these items should only be used for your ceremonies)
- A clear calcite or clear quartz crystal
- A small plate (again, use this plate only for your ceremonies)
- Filtered water or spring water
- A No. 2 pencil

- Parchment paper
- Olive oil
- Honey
- Brown sugar
- Cinnamon powder
- Cayenne powder
- Chamomile flowers (or the petals of your favorite flower)

Reflect on something you would like the strength of the high-noon sun to help you manifest. Write this down on the paper with the pencil. Hold a clear calcite or clear quartz in your hands, and place your intentions into the crystal. Place filtered water, or preferably spring water, in the glass or bowl, and put the crystal inside the bowl. Then place the bowl on top of the parchment paper. Leave the bowl outside or on a windowsill for one hour of the daily zenith of the sun, one hour ahead or after, ideally for 3 days, to get the full stamina of the high noon sun.

After the third day, place the parchment paper on top of a small platter. Cover the paper in olive oil, and then place brown sugar on top of the paper, along with cinnamon and cayenne powder, and finally place the flower petals at the very top. Place the plate on your altar or in a special place. When your intention comes to be, remove the contents from the plate and bury them.

## *Making a Flower Essence*

To make a flower essence, I recommend using flowers that you are growing in your garden, or one of the Mexica's favorite "power" flowers, marigolds—they love the sun and can thrive in the high noon sun. Marigolds also have numerous medicinal and spiritual benefits: they strengthen the auric fields and immune system; help digestion; enhance intuition; increase the chances of lucid and prophetic dreams; reduce inflammation; eliminate free radicals in the body; repel bugs naturally; and have antiseptic properties.

For this rite you will need:

- A plain lidded glass bowl or jar that can hold twelve ounces of water
- Small one-ounce glass bottle with a euro dropper lid
- Distilled water
- Brandy
- Three or four fresh flowers, preferably marigolds

Do this ritual starting at noon on a sunny day. Place distilled water into a bowl. Connect with the flowers, and ask for permission to take some blossoms. After permission is granted, snip three to six blossoms, allowing them to fall into the bowl of water. Place the bowl of water undisturbed for one hour before and after the daily zenith of the sun.

Fill the dropper bottle with brandy. With the euro dropper, add two drops of the water from the bowl, and seal the bottle. Pour the remaining water from the bowl with the blossoms, near the base of the flowers that were picked.

The flower essence can typically last for two years if it is kept in the refrigerator. Before using your flower essence, remember to strengthen it by being grateful that it is infused with the gifts of the flowers and the sun's high noon sacred essence energies.

Here are some ways to use the flower essence:

- Take 2 or 3 drops under the tongue or in a glass of water
- Add 20 to 40 drops in a bath
- Add 2 to 10 drops in misters
- Infuse 2 to 10 drops into your favorite lotion
- Place 2 or 3 drops into your morning green drink

## WORKING WITH THE ENERGIES OF AFTERNOON

For the ancient Mexica, the period of afternoon began approximately an hour past high noon. We can use the waning of the sun's stamina to help decrease something, cleanse, cloak and camouflage information, lessen uncertainty or confusion, and sharpen spiritual discernment.

The focus of the recommended rites will be on releasing and decreasing, and on obtaining greater clarity. When we release or reduce blocks, dense energies, and things that no longer serve us, we can obtain greater clarity and focus, so along with focusing on releasing and decreasing, you can also ask for greater clarity and focus.

Here are some sacred Mexica and Maya items, activities, and deities associated with the afternoon and these energies:

- Shamanic breathwork
- Ritual dancing or singing
- Ceremonial offerings, such as lighting a charcoal tablet and placing copal on it; offering copal
- Honoring our elders
- Decreasing
- Cleansing
- Cloaking and camouflaging information and energies
- Solar deities, Cihuateteo*

## *Afternoon Intention to Release or Decrease*

If you are choosing to decrease or release something in your life, this afternoon intention is perfect. You can tailor it to last a few minutes or longer.

Close your eyes. Connect with your breath. Take a deep inhale through the nose and exhale out of the nose. Repeat 3 times. Then take a deep inhale and exhale out of the mouth. Repeat 3 times. Alternate these cycles until you feel relaxed. Then connect with the waning sun: visualize him, send loving energy to him, and thank him for taking whatever you are releasing into the Underworld when he sets.

I do not recommend mantras stating the intention to release or decrease something; avoid attracting what you are trying to release by focusing on it repeatedly. Just keep it simple, and focus on your intention to decrease or

*Cihuateteo are warrior goddesses of the Mexica who died in childbirth. They are bare breasted, carry a shield and spears, and have wild hair and skirts fastened with a snake belt.[26]

release. I recommend mantras for what you are choosing, not for things that you want to release or decrease.

## *Journey for Releasing and Gaining Greater Clarity*

Since the focus is on decreasing and releasing, I am going to recommend releasing breathwork exercises to purify the body and help you get into a trance meditative state. You can do all of the breathwork exercises, or just the ones you prefer.

### Cupping Hands and Releasing Breathwork

Start by cupping your hands over the mouth, and take a deep inhale. Open your hands, and exhale quickly and vigorously 3 times, pulling in your abdomen to help you exhale and release. Repeat this exercise 3 to 7 times.

### Mental and Emotional Release Breathwork

Take a deep inhale while slowly rolling the shoulders up and squeezing them. Move the shoulders back, pull the chest out, and make a sharp "SHUI" sound. Exhale softly, release squeezing the chest and shoulders. Repeat this exercise 3 to 7 times.

### Primal Releasing Breathwork

This breathwork exercise is a primal release, so let yourself be primal in the release. Inhale and gently shake the body while making a loud and long "AH" sound. Release by moving the shoulders back, pulling the chest out, and exhaling with a sharp "HA" sound. Continue the exhale softly, releasing chest and shoulders. Repeat this exercise 3 to 7 times.

### Journey to Release and Gain Clarity

Turn your attention to your breath. Connect with your I Am presence and journey into your sacred heart through the violet fires of transmutation of dense energies, and the white fires of resurrection and divine remembrance of our infinite potential. (Follow the instructions on pages 71 and 72 for connecting with your I Am and journeying within the sacred heart.)

See yourself at the entrance of a mountain cave, soaking up the sun's afternoon rays that are entering the cave. Caves in ancient Mesoamerica had multiple meanings and associations and often were identified with the space through which the sun entered to journey through the Underworld at night.

Allow the afternoon sun and cave to facilitate your intentions, and thank them for it. State an invocation in this space along the lines of: "In the name of my I Am presence, I accept that the release [or decrease] of . . . has happened [or is happening] in and with impeccability. I move forward with greater clarity and focus."

Exit the mountain cave through your sacred heart. Visualize yourself in the sacred white fires of purification and resurrection, and then in the violet fires; listen to the sacred fire angels congratulate you for releasing that which no longer serves you. Then take 6 deep inhales and exhales, inhaling into the nose and exhaling out of the mouth. Gently rub your thighs with your hands, coming back fully present and grounded.

## MORE ELABORATE AFTERNOON RITES

### ◎ *Herbal Incense: Decrease and Release and Bringing in More Clarity*

For this rite you will need:

- A charcoal tablet
- A steel or glazed brazier
- Wooden stick matches
- A resealable plastic bag
- A container with a lid (optional)
- Any or all of the following herbs: basil, lemon balm, peppermint, or sage

If you buy the herbs fresh, let them dry in a dark place. All of these herbs help to clear, decrease, and release, and here are some of their other gifts:

**Basil** calms tempers and clears dense energies, induces mental clarity, clears anguish and sadness, and opens up pathways.

**Lemon balm** aids in releasing judgment, ensures justice and right action, enhances powers of manifestation, and deepens the spiritual connection with our divine presence.

**Peppermint** purifies, enhances prosperity, and improves clarity and focus.

**Sage** purifies, enhances great fortune, develops intuition, and invites longevity.

Run your hands in running water, setting the intention that the water cleanse your hands. Get your herbs, and thank them for helping to clear dense energies and bring in clarity. If you would like to clear specific energies, or would like greater clarity about something, tailor your gratitude toward those intentions.

Take one leaf of each herb and place it into the bag, continuing until the bag is at least one-tenth full. Gently crumble the leaves inside the bag, allowing the oils of the herbs to be released on the crumbled leaves. (I have chosen these particular herbs because they tend to crumble easily if gently pressed.) Try not to crumble them into a powder, just enough to create an incense mix.

Connect with the afternoon sun by closing your eyes and visualizing the waning sun heading toward its setting. (You don't necessarily have to do this ceremony in the afternoon, but if you can, it tends to make the connection with the afternoon sun easier.) Then light the charcoal tablet with a match and place it on the brazier.

Place your fresh incense on the charcoal tablet. Use your hands, a feather, or feather fan to lift the smoke to your face and then body. After you have smudged yourself, allow yourself to go into a trance with a repetitive drumbeat or breathwork or by simply setting the intention, and softly focus on what you would like clarity on. Whatever visions you may get, trust that the herbs and afternoon sun will bring more clarity, even outside of this ritual. Once you feel complete, let the charcoal burn out naturally, and close the ceremony with a closing prayer of gratitude. If you have any of your incense left, place it in a container or leave it in the resealable bag.

### *White Fire Limpia to Clear Energies and Open Pathways*

For this rite you will need:

- A pot with a handle, preferably a stainless-steel or cast-iron pot (again, tools for limpias should never be used for cooking, eating, or drinking—they are sacred cleansing items and should be placed in a separate space, out of reach, so they are not mistakenly used)
- A couple of handfuls of plain Epsom salt
- Rubbing alcohol
- Dry herbs—all herbs have phenomenal cleansing gifts, including any of the herbs listed for the previous rite
- Wooden stick matches
- A No. 2 pencil
- A piece of paper

Before using the herbs for the limpia, take a moment to connect with their spirit essence, and share your intention and prayers with them. Remember to thank them for their assistance; doing so strengthens intentions and can build wonderful plant allies.

Allow yourself to go into a slight trance state with breathwork, repetitive drumming, or simple intention. Connect with the afternoon sun by closing your eyes and visualizing the waning sun. Request that the sun help you clear or decrease energies, open up pathways for you, and take these unwanted energies into the Underworld on its night journey. In this relaxed state, write down your intention on the plain paper with the pencil.

After writing down your intention, place the alcohol and Epsom salt in the pot. Make sure the rubbing alcohol covers the Epsom salt so that it will light on fire. The amount of alcohol needed is usually about a quarter cup, but it may be less or more, depending on the size of the pot. Carefully throw the match into the pot. Throw your paper, and then your herbs, into the fire.

The herbs serve as an offering to the fire. State your intention, and watch the fire, until the fire goes out. As you are stating your intention, remember to thank the spirit of the fire, the herbs, and the waning sun for helping you to manifest your intention.

---

### My Own Healing from the High Noon Sun

I learned of the amazing healing and restorative properties of the high noon sun after a catastrophic injury I experienced in May 2005. (I discuss the accident and my healing journey in greater detail in my first book, *Cleansing Rites of Curanderismo*.)

I was in Las Vegas for a work convention, but I did not want to gamble afterward; I wanted to do something peaceful and go hiking. I decided to go to Red Rock Canyon in Las Vegas. During my hike, I found a spot that pulled me and went into a very deep journey. When I came out of it, I realized that four hours had passed, although it only felt like fifteen minutes. Unfortunately, I jumped up, panicked, and did not take time to ground myself. I slipped and fell over thirty feet.

The fall resulted in a skull fracture, brain hemorrhage, left acromioclavicular joint separation, two fractured vertebrae, shattered coccyx, three fractures in the left leg, and a right leg fractured down from the knee, with my bones coming out of my heel. I also experienced severe osteomyelitis, lost half the bones in my right ankle, and almost had my right foot amputated. I was told I would be in pain the rest of my life, and if I walked again, it would likely be with some kind of assistance.

In the hospital I decided to finally fully embrace my *don* (healing gift from God), step into my power, and learn to stop doubting intuitive divine guidance (the most difficult of all).

When I finally came home, I was still in a wheelchair, but I was able to start using a walker, even though I could not place pressure on my right foot. It was recommended that I use the wheelchair most of the time. I knew I had to do something to keep the energy moving in my right leg and body. I also wanted to get off the pain medications I was on. Along with using my other limpia healing practices, I was guided to recharge myself with the energies of the high noon sun and clear the energetic blockages caused by the fractures, surgeries, and lack of movement.

By this time, I was deep in my shamanic dreamwork practices. One night I dreamed that I had a discussion with Tonatiuh, who told me to replenish myself with twenty minutes of sunbathing and placing crystals on my energy centers, increasing the time incrementally.

I got seven crystals that correlated with the colors of my chakras, placed them on my chakras, and sunbathed almost every day for three months. During this time I also journeyed to Xochicalli and thanked the sun for healing me and moving the energy in my body.

After the first two weeks of this practice, I no longer needed the pain medications and was free from any kind of pain. The divine guidance I received during this daily sunbathing and journeying to Xochicalli were mind-blowing. I received an immense amount of information for healing recipes and even opened my door to see a few clients during my recovery process. After my second to last surgery, I finally was given permission to place pressure on my right foot. I walked with a completely normal gait in less than two weeks, although I had not walked for almost a year, and remained 100 percent pain-free.

# 5

# Sunset, Dusk, and Nightfall

## *Rites of Transformation*

For the ancient Mexica and Maya, sunset was one of the most important ritual times to watch the sky and perform divination.[1] It marked a period of transformation into darkness and night. At this time their beloved sun began its journey into the Underworld to undergo different metamorphoses. As I explain in *Curanderismo Soul Retrieval*, their Underworld was generally believed to contain regenerative life forces, but at the same time it was a dreaded place of decay and disease. The Underworld was also thought to have nine different levels, each with its own distinct tests, trials, and tribulations.[2] If one passed these tests, the Underworld could be a place of transformation and rebirth.[3]

The sun's journey and transformation through the Underworld required assistance from beings that could journey through these dangerous yet transformative realms. Offerings and ritual singing and playing of instruments were used to aid the sun through its journey, as well as to invoke and interact with deities and ancestors.

When the light in the sky began dwindling from twilight to dusk, preparations for night ceremonies began. The people typically stopped their daytime ritual dancing and singing (unless the ceremonies were going on for more than a day). When it became night, sacrificed warriors transformed into stars. Rites to change challenging cycles were performed; marriages took place; seniors engaged in ritual drinking; fire shamans engaged in ceremonial bathing; and the dead were ritually honored. The sun deity transformed into a jaguar at night and roamed the Underworld as a Lord of Night.

To determine the hour of the night and conduct divination, a number of celestial bodies were observed, including Venus, the Pleiades, the Milky Way, Orion's Belt, the Scorpius constellation, the North Star, the Dippers, and the Gemini constellation—Castor and Pollux.[4]

## SUNSET

*Path to Transformation*

Sunset signaled a path toward transformation for the sun and for the Earth's inhabitants. The underlying theme was the cycle of death and rebirth. During his journey into the Underworld, the Red Xolotl, depicted in the Codex Borgia with canine feet and claws, a canine mouth, and a distended eye, carried the night sun deity on his back through the Underworld.[5] The Mexica believed that dogs guided the sun, along with the deceased, through the Underworld, so the canine features of Xolotl likely play on this belief.[6]

Page 39 of the Codex Borgia depicts Stripe Eye (one of the text's central characters) and Xochipilli flying downward in a red disk. They are carrying an olla or drum and a long trumpet (see plate 8). They are singing to cheer the sun as it enters the Underworld.[7]

On page 40, the sun appears as a great black sun in a birth-giving pose with spots and bumps on the hands and feet identifying him as Nanahuatzin, the man who became the sun (from the creation mythology of the sun discussed in chapter 1; see plate 9). His eyes are open, and he appears to be singing or speaking, while nine black males in Quetzalcoatl garb cut hearts out of the nine sun disks on his body.[8] The night sun is being sacrificed nine times but in the morning will be resurrected. These nine deaths reflect the trials of the sun as it journeys through the Underworld.[9] Ritual singing or poetic speaking, associated with Xochipilli, seemed to be critical for facilitating the sun's movement through the levels of the Underworld to be reborn anew.

Sunset also marked the time when at the Great Festival of the Dead, Xocotl Uetzi (also known as the Hueymiccaihuitl), the men climbed a *xocotl* in a race to get to the top and knock down a figurine (made of *tzoalli,* or amaranth seed) of Otontecuhtli, a god of death.[10] The xocotl was a tall tree, at least 110 to 140 feet tall, which the Mexica treated as a sacred being and adorned with jewelry, featherwork, and flowers.[11]

The winner cut off the head of Otontecuhtli and was allowed to keep a piece of the figurine in his home for one solar year.[12] This figurine was believed to be imbued with the sacred essence energy of Otontecuhtli, so keeping a piece of it was a great honor.

Sunset was also a period for making offerings to the deities. The youths who served in the temple of Huitzilopochtli engaged in *tlenemactli,* an incense ceremony, at sunset, midnight, and dawn.[13] For Toxcatl, the primary feast for Tezcatlipoca, young women took large clay plates filled with tzoalli formed in shape of skulls and crossbones to an image of the god.[14] On the day before the Ochpaniztli feast (the day of sweeping) held for Toci, the shamans blew conch shells and horns and beat the drums to announce the start of the statewide practice of offerings made by all mothers. Each mother carried offerings in her hands and on her back and left them at all the temples of her ward. Fathers would light the way with pine torches.

After leaving offerings at the temples, the people went to the great temple of Tenochtitlan to make the final offering. The shamans purified them with limpias to cleanse the women of childbearing. This rite, among other purposes, likely cleared any difficulties that may have arisen from childbirth, and possibly opened pathways for more children.[15]

For the Maya, at sunset the sun deity K'inich Ahau began his journey into the Underworld, during which he was carried by a centipede.[16]

Because it aided the sun in this journey, the centipede was closely associated with death and the Underworld, as well as with the cycle of death and rebirth. By day, centipedes hide under stones or logs on the ground, beneath loose bark, in rotting wood, in caves, and in similar subterranean regions of darkness.[17] A late Classic stucco vessel depicts a singing musician with rattles in a centipede's mouth, a scene that may relate to the ritual importance of music for conjuring and communicating with the deceased.[18]

Many of the Classic Maya likely also started the ritual calendar (*tzolk'in*) day at sunset followed by the solar calendar (*ha'b*) day at sunrise.[19] Mesoamerican scholar Alexandre Tokovinine asserts that the dates at Classic sites—Palenque (sarcophagus in the Temple of the Inscriptions at Palenque that reports the Calendar Round date of Kan B'ahlam II's death), La Sufricaya (painted inscription in the palace), and Copan (Stela 63)—point to an alternative way of counting ha'b solar days that has something to do with Teotihuacan influence or Classic Maya perception of Teotihuacan, wherein the ha'b calendar day began at sunset and the tzolk'in began at sunrise.[20] Ethnographic data also suggests that counting days from sunset to sunset may be a living tradition in some Maya communities. For speakers of Mam, Cakchiquel of Jacaltenango, Kanjobal of Santa Eulalia, and the Tzotzil of San Pedro Chenalho, the solar day begins at sunset and not at sunrise as for other Maya groups.[21] Tokovinine further asserts that the unusual dates in the Classic Maya inscriptions were all commissioned by individuals with some connection to Teotihuacan, which may have influenced the recordings of their day beginning at sunset.[22]

## DUSK

*Preparations for Transformation*

Dusk marked the end-of-day ceremonies and involved preparatory rites for the night. For the Teotleco feast, the arrival of the gods, the shamans of Huitzilopochtli carried, with awe and reverence, a large and beautifully decorated tub containing a specially prepared corn dough to the top of the temple of Huitzilopochtli. At dusk, they left the dough in front of the image of Huitzilopochtli to see if he would leave his footprint on it, signifying that he would come to be born on Earth and the old gods would arrive on Earth the next day.[23] The shamans checked periodically throughout the night to see if Huitzilopochtli had left his footprint on the dough.[24] Dusk and nighttime were transitional periods during which supernatural beings could cross over into the physical realm and leave their imprints.

For numerous day ceremonies, participants would chant and dance all day until dusk to set the stage for the pivotal evening ceremony.[25] For the Mexica Xochipaina (first flowers of the season) rite, the pipiltzin came out in their finest attire, resplendent jewelry, and featherwork, and with flowers in their hands and on their necks and heads. They danced all day. Wearing the flowers during the day in the ritual dance was part of the offering to Huitzilopochtli. At dusk, they took the flower garlands to his temple as an offering of the season's first flowers.[26]

## NIGHTFALL

### *Regenerative Transformation*

At nightfall, ancestors and deities had greater access to the earthly planes and were fed by offerings, including ritual dancing, singing, food, and fire. At the Mexica festival of Toxcatl, held for the deity Tezcatlipoca, at nightfall the women danced in procession carrying their paper petitions painted in designs with liquid rubber and left them at the deity's temple. The rest of the night they sang and danced the Toxcatl leap.[27] In the month Uei Tecuilhuitl, when the poor were fed for eight days, at nightfall, the pipiltzin, adorned in rich vestments and lavish jewelry began singing and dancing in a plaza with numerous lit pine torches and continued until nine o'clock.[28] At nightfall for twenty days during the month of Panquetzaliztli, they sang a song for Huitzilopochtli and danced until the conch shells were blown, slightly before midnight.[29]

At nightfall of the fifth day of the Quecholli feast, which was dedicated to the dead, the Mexica made offerings to the dead. They made small spears out of oak and applied a little bit of resin, probably copal, on each one. They bound four of the spears together with four pine torches and made bundles. The bundles were placed where the dead had been buried, with two sweet tamales laid on each bundle. The people stayed at the burial site all day. At nightfall, they burned the bundles for the dead, so the smoke and fire carried the fragrant smell of the oak, sweet tamales, and resin.[30]

Another Mexica type of transformation that took place at night was weddings. Courting would begin in the morning. A group of older women related to the suitor would go to the home of the maiden for a few days to solicit her parents in the hopes of an amicable marriage.[31] If an agreement was made, at dawn of the wedding day, the couple's families celebrated with them, eating food and drinking chocolate. At midday the elders entered and joined the celebration. At dusk, when there was still a little sun, the couple was placed before the hearth, and gifts were presented to them. When the sun was no longer visible, at nightfall, the elderly matchmakers tied the couple together with the corner of the man's cape and the woman's shift, and married them.[32]

In the Central Mexican codices, the night sky was typically depicted as a dark grey field patterned with black disks, tiny black spots, and night eyes, which were stars. This same patterned field also represented night or simply darkness.[33] Along with deities and ancestors, these night eyes may also have been seen as sacrificed warriors. The Mexica believed that souls of sacrificed warriors transformed into stars.[34]

Ritual drinking of pulque also took place at nightfall. The Mexica associated pulque with the moon and night, and although they highly revered it, they restricted drinking it for the general populace, except for ceremonial reasons. The drinking of pulque was welcome during many nighttime ceremonies.[35]

According to Diego de Landa, the Maya knew what time it was by observing Venus, the Pleiades, and the constellation Gemini at night.[36]

For the Maya, nightfall was when the sun deity, K'inich Ahau, transformed into a jaguar deity and roamed the Underworld as one of the Lords of Night.[37] The night sun deity was typically depicted with attributes of a jaguar and the color black.[38] The aspect of K'inich Ahau that did not become a jaguar was carried by a centipede through the Underworld.[39]

The Maya Cauac yearbearer, comprising thirteen years, were generally understood as unfortunate years, which would include many deaths, hot spells, lack of rain, and plagues of birds and ants that would destroy crops.[40] In order to reverse the misfortune associated with these years, the Maya walked over hot coals at the New Year Cauac ceremonies at nightfall. This was regarded as an offering to ease or transfigure the misfortunes of the Cauac years.[41]

Diego de Landa also tells of nightfall ceremonial offerings that were made by the Postclassic Maya from the province of Maní. These were intended to inspire the serpent deity Kukulcán* to descend from the Upperworld to Earth on the sixteenth of the solar month Xul. On this day, all chiefs, shamans, and numerous other people, who had been fasting, assembled at Maní. At nightfall they began a procession from the house of the principal chief to the temple of Kukulcán. Upon arriving, they said their prayers and set the banners on top of the temple. The people placed their images on trees, probably to renew the images' sacred essence energy. They offered and lit a New Fire—marking a new cycle that was blessed by Kukulcán—abstained from salt or chili peppers, and burned copal. They began ritual dancing and continued their

*De Landa seems to associate the arrival of Kukulcán with the figure known as Topiltzin-Quetzalcoatl, the mythical Toltec ruler who was disgraced and felt compelled to leave the Toltec homeland of Tula (900–1150 CE). There are different explanations of why he left Tula and where he went afterward. Due to De Landa's indication that this ceremony was practiced in Mayapan (1220–1440 CE), which mirrored the architecture of Chichén Itzá, it seems more likely that this rite welcomed in the feathered serpent deity Kukulcán or Ehecatl-Quetzalcoatl, who predated the mythical human Toltec ruler Topiltzin-Quetzalcoatl, who apparently was later deified.

prayers, copal offerings, and festivities for five days. They believed that Kukulcán descended on the last of those five days to receive their sacrifices, penances, and offerings.[42]

# RECOMMENDED RITES

## Sunset, Dusk, and Nightfall

### WORKING WITH THE ENERGIES OF SUNSET

The ancient Mexica and Maya saw sunset as an ideal time to draw on transformative energies. Sunset signaled a time when their beloved sun would begin its journey into the Underworld to undergo trials and tribulations. Their ceremonial games and offerings to the dead indicate that they likely believed that the veils between the living and those that resided in other worlds began to thin at sunset. This period of time is ideal to reflect on transformation and release.

Sunset is when the sun is .57° below the horizon and can create unique atmospheric conditions such as beautiful orange and red hues in the sky. Dusk is the darkest part of evening twilight and occurs just before the minimum brightness of the night sky. It typically takes seventy to a hundred minutes from sunset to nightfall. When working with the energies of sunset, I recommend checking the internet to determine when sunset will take place where you live. The peak of the sunset energies are at the start of sunset and approximately forty minutes thereafter.

Inspired by ancient Mexica and Maya thought, the following sacred items, activities, and night sun deity enable us to work with the energies naturally flowing at sunset:

- Breathwork exercises for releasing and closing the energies of the day
- Ritual singing and spoken words that invite release and transformation

- Nurturing activities that inspire release and transformation
- Ritual art projects such as making *calaveras* (skulls) or calavera face painting
- Contemplative writing or visualization projects focusing on release and transformation
- Copal offerings
- Fire limpia rituals
- Sunset solar deity, Tlalchitonatiuh*

## *Shamanic Breathwork and Movement to Release Stress*

If you can do this exercise outside at sunset, this is perfect, as it will be much easier to connect with the energies of the setting sun. If this is not possible, simply set the intention of connecting to the setting sun to release emotional or mental weight or stress. Thank the sun for taking any unwanted stress with him during his journey into the Underworld.

Sit with your back straight, either in a chair or in butterfly pose, with the soles of your feet touching and your legs creating a diamond shape. Turn your attention to your breath. Experience the air traveling into your nose, expanding your lungs and oxygenating every cell of your body, going down to your feet. Slowly exhale out of the nose. After you feel that you are in a slight meditative state, engage in the neck tilt, allowing any emotional or mental weight to be released and carried away by the setting sun.

### Neck Tilt and Scanning the Body

While doing this exercise, scan and be mindful of the neck and shoulders. See if you are holding any tension in these areas. If you are, release it with your breath and out into the setting sun.

Inhale, tilting the head to the left side of the shoulder, hold your breath,

*Tlalchitonatiuh is associated with medicine bundles that contain sacred items relating to the cycles of death and rebirth, crossbones, black body paint, facial markings, crocodile skin, red sphere at the solar plexus (refer to pages 30–31 for more information).

and allow the right shoulder to stretch. Gently move the head back to the center while slowly exhaling.

Inhale, tilting the head to the bottom left side of the shoulder, drawing the chin into the chest, hold your breath, and allow the right shoulder to stretch. Gently move the head back to the center while slowly exhaling.

Inhale, tilting the head to the right side of the shoulder, hold your breath, and allow the left shoulder to stretch. Gently move the head back to the center while slowly exhaling.

Inhale, tilting the head to the bottom right side of the shoulder, drawing the chin into the chest. Hold your breath, and allow the left shoulder to stretch. Gently move the head back to the center while slowly exhaling.

Once you are done with the head tilt, turn your attention again to your breath and the setting sun. Thank the sun once again for taking any unwanted weight or stress from you.

## *Journaling and Mantras: Transmuting Self-Limiting Beliefs*

This rite is to aid in changing self-limiting beliefs and thoughts with the help of the setting sun. Get a piece of paper, and draw a line in the middle. Reflect on your day or week, and on one side of the paper, write down any self-limiting or negative beliefs, thoughts, or statements that you have had about yourself that day or week. Keep in mind that after the breathwork exercises, you will be addressing each item and changing that statement or belief into a positive one, so make sure you begin with a number that you will have time to address in this rite.

After you feel complete with writing down self-limiting beliefs, connect with the setting sun by visualizing the sun setting in your mind's eye. Cup your hands over your face, take a big inhale, hold the breath, and release the breath while moving your hands down in prayer position toward the center of your chest, the heart chakra. When doing so, set the intention of balancing your energy and aligning it with that of the setting sun in your heart chakra.

Reflect on each item, and transfigure it into a positive "I am" or "I can" statement. Write them down on the other side of the paper. Let these statements be your new mantras, until you no longer have those self-limiting beliefs or thoughts.

## MORE ELABORATE SUNSET RITES

### ◎ *Fire Limpias: Creating Sacred Spaces of Transmutation*

This limpia rite is intended to infuse a physical space, such as a bedroom, office, yoga studio, or living room, with the energy of transmutation, cleansing, and renewal. This limpia involves fire, with which ancient Mesoamerican shamans conjured and communicated with supernatural beings. Fire was used for different kinds of divination work; it could house supernatural beings or the deceased; and it cleansed, renewed, and vivified the sacred essence energy of physical spaces and ritual objects.

In limpias, triangles strengthen intentions. You will be creating a triangle with four points. Three points mark the apexes of the triangle; the fourth point is the center, where you will be sitting. The objects you can work with include candles, charcoal tablets and resin, white fires, and a firepit and wood. Start by doing an initial cleanse of the space by smudging it with a bundle of dry herbs; remember, all herbs have cleansing properties.

If you would like to work with candles, you will need four white candles and four stick matches. You can work with any size candle, but whatever size you choose, you should let it burn out on its own; do not snuff it out. Use one match per candle.

If you would like to work with charcoal tablets and resin, you will need four steel or glazed braziers, four charcoal tablets, copal, and four stick matches. Use one match per charcoal tablet. Once the charcoal is lit, place the copal on it. Let the charcoal burn out naturally.

If you would like to work with white fires, you will need four pots, Epsom salt, rubbing alcohol, dry herbs, four stick matches, four firepits, and wood (see pages 81–82 for more information). The firepits and wood can be any size. It is a good idea to feed the fire with offerings, such as dry herbs or flowers. If you can, let the wood become ash and go out naturally. If this is not possible, pour water on the wood, and stir it around with a shovel to make sure the fire is extinguished.

Once you have created your triangle and are in the middle, face one of the points of the triangle, which will be the focal point of the triangle. Connect with energies of the setting sun by visualizing him in your mind's eye. Ignite the frame first, and start by igniting the left-hand bottom side, right, focal point, and then the center. Sit down and get comfortable. Finally, use spoken words, intention, drumming, dancing, breathwork, singing, or drawing, as well as the energies of the setting sun, to activate the space with the energies of transmutation, cleansing, and renewal. I have done this for my bedroom and experience incredibly profound prophetic dreams and clearing. Once you feel that the activation is complete, say a closing prayer of gratitude for the fire, setting sun, and any other tools you used for this activation, and then leave the center.

The energy will generally hold strong for 7 to 14 days after the completion of this rite. But it will fade more quickly if many people share the space with you who were not a part of creating the space energy signature, or if you or others continually come into the space with dense or toxic energy.

## WORKING WITH THE ENERGIES OF DUSK

The energies of dusk are ideal for preparing night rituals or for ending day ceremonies. As the sun goes down and descends into the Underworld, the transformative energies of night take a greater hold. The peak of dusk energies are approximately thirty minutes before nightfall. According to the ancient Mexica and Maya, at this time the centipede or dog was now carrying the sun into the Underworld. Ideal activities and sacred items for tapping into and utilizing dusk energies include:

- Ending day or afternoon ceremonies
- Preparing for a night ceremony
- Ritual offerings of tobacco or copal
- Rites for connecting and journeying with animal spirit guides
- Centipedes: images and related items
- Dogs as a symbol of loyalty and guidance: images and related items

## *Gazing into Trance: Connecting with an Animal Spirit Guide*

At dusk, go outside and connect with the skies. At this point, the sun has gone below the horizon and light still in the sky is very dim. Night is approaching—this is the cusp of transformation. Have your eyes one-tenth open and gaze into the sky; this helps to induce a trance state. You know you are gazing if you can see the tip of your nose or your eyelashes. If you are unable to go outside, connect mentally with the sun at dusk, then practice gazing into sacred geometrical images, such as the Mexica Sun Stone, a mandala, or a Sri Yantra. Gazing into sacred geometrical images enables us to access higher states of consciousness.

Inhale through the nose and exhale out of the nose 3 times, slowly and mindfully. Then inhale through the nose and exhale out of the mouth 3 times, again slowly and mindfully.

In this light trance, ask an animal to come forward to help you to discover and change something about yourself. Let a vision of an animal come into your mind's eye, and now travel with the animal into your life. If the animal flies, soar with the animal. If it walks or runs on four legs, do so; if it slithers, then slither with it. However it moves, move with the animal, and let yourself be one with the wisdom of the animal. See your life through the animal's essence as an objective and detached observer to help you discover or change something about yourself.

When you feel complete, take 6 deep inhales through the nose and exhales out of the mouth, and thank the animal, the dusk, and the night sun for sharing their wisdom with you.

## MORE ELABORATE DUSK RITES

### *Ceremonial Tobacco Offerings for Transformation*

This rite petitions divine aid for changing or transforming something in your life with sacred tools and offerings used by the Mexica and Maya for this time of day. For this rite you will need:

- A plate
- Tobacco (preferably organic)
- A 7-day white candle and glass to hold it
- Brown paper (from a trash bag is fine)
- A No. 2 pencil
- Honey
- Wooden stick matches
- Smudging herbs (or something to cleanse the space, such as white fire, charcoal tablets with resin, or rose water)

Cleanse the space for this ceremony with a bundle of dry herbs, or with your preferred method of cleansing spaces. Connect with the dusk skies and the energy of transformation from day into night. Go into a slight trance state by focusing on your breath, repetitive drumming, or any other way you find effective.

Focus on what you would like to change with divine aid. Narrow it down to one sentence. Write down that sentence 21 times on the brown paper with the pencil. Write it down in the affirmative, starting with a statement of gratitude. Some examples may be:

- Thank you, all that is, for your divine aid in . . . (state your choice).
- I Am That I Am, thank you for . . . (state your choice).
- Thank you (use a name that reflects divinity for you, such as God, Nature, or the name of a saint) for your help in . . . (state your choice).

On the plate, use the tobacco to create a circle with a cross inside it.

Place the petition in the middle of the cross, put a spiral of honey on the petition, and place the 7-day candle on top of the petition.

At dusk, light the candle with the matchstick. State your intention (what you wrote) 21 times. Then let the candle go out naturally. After it does, throw away the glass that held the 7-day candle. Make a hole in the Earth, scrape the items that are on the plate (tobacco, brown paper, and honey) into the hole, and bury it. Thank the night sun and Mother Earth for their help.

## WORKING WITH THE ENERGIES OF NIGHTFALL

The energies of nightfall embody transformation and facilitate metamorphoses. Many of us shy away from change, but the truth is, change is constant. Flowing gracefully with change and using it as an opportunity to become a better version of ourselves, to elevate our self-awareness, and for spiritual growth can help us to ride the waves of change with greater ease and creativity; it can also expand our zest for life.

The following sacred activities, items, and night sun deity enable us to access the energies of nightfall or the beginning of night.

- Ceremonies involving movement, dancing, and word play to move stagnant energies and flow with transformation
- Rites committing yourself to self-love or loving someone else
- Rites inviting change and transformation
- Pictures or items associated with the jaguar
- Copal or tobacco offerings
- Rites to honor the deceased and ancestors
- K'inich Ahau, as a Lord of Night*

*See pages 35–36 for more information on K'inich Ahau.

## ◎ *Shamanic Breathwork, Toning, and Glossolalia for Regenerative Transformation*

This rite helps to release and transform energy with free-flowing *bijas* (Sanskrit for "seed mantras")* that stimulate the seven principal chakras (refer to pages 73–74 for chakras and the associations):

**Root chakra:** UH (guttural sound)
**Sacral chakra:** OO
**Solar plexus chakra:** OH
**Heart chakra:** AH
**Throat chakra:** EYE
**Third eye chakra:** AYE or AUM
**Crown chakra:** EE or OM

Let yourself get comfortable, and connect with nightfall, the moon, sky, and the stars. Root yourself into the Earth by visualizing a ruby grounding cord dropping down from your tailbone and connecting to the heart of the Earth. Begin by toning the seed sounds. After one cycle of toning the sounds, begin to utter the sounds, and let each sound emerge and create words; speak in tongues. Examples can include: Uhtatchat, OOseetat, OHseenat, AHlat, EYElat, AYEhom, EEhom. Let the energy of mysticism, change, and regenerative transformation infuse you as you are speaking in tongues.

Once you feel charged with the energy of regenerative transformation, let it continue to run through your body by doing the following circuitry breathwork:

Take a deep inhale. Hold your breath, tilt your head back, open your eyes, and close your eyes. Bring your head back to center, and exhale. Repeat 3 times.

Take a deep inhale, squeeze your shoulders, and hold your breath for about 30 seconds. Exhale, and release the squeeze. Repeat 3 times.

---

*Certain sounds are experiences of energy in their own right. The sounds and bijas I suggest do not represent things or concepts; rather, they are energetic frequencies that stimulate the chakras. Buenaflor, *Curanderismo Soul Retrieval,* 44.

Take a deep inhale, and make a tight fist with both hands. Hold your breath for about 30 seconds, exhale, and release the fist. Repeat 3 times.

Take a deep inhale, squeeze your buttocks, and hold your breath for about 30 seconds. Exhale, and release the squeeze. Repeat 3 times.

Take a deep inhale, and curl your toes in tight. Hold your breath for about 30 seconds, exhale, and release the squeezing of your toes. Repeat 3 times.

Now set the intention of releasing any energy that is not yours out and down through your grounding cord. Thank the night sun, stars, skies, and moon for facilitating a regenerative transformation for you.

### *Shamanic Dancing Exercise for Transfiguration*

Engage in rhythmic breathing: 3 breaths in, then 3 breaths out. Have your eyes one-tenth open, so you are gazing, enhancing the trance state. While listening to deep repetitive drumbeats, do a:

- Light trot, standing in one place, gently shaking your shoulders and hands
- Light trot, moving clockwise 3 times in a circle; the circle can be as wide or small as your space allows
- Light trot, spiraling to the center of the circle
- Light trot, moving counterclockwise 3 times in a circle

After dancing, use the closing breathwork exercises given above, and set the intention of releasing any and all energy that is not yours out your grounding cord. Once again, thank the night sun, stars, sky, and moon for transfiguring unwanted energies for you.

## MORE ELABORATE NIGHTFALL RITES

### *Shamanic Dreamwork: Regeneration and Deepening Self-Awareness and Spiritual Growth*

Dream incubation and preparation for shamanic dreamwork is an ideal nightfall practice to tap into universal energies and forces and into forms of intelligence that live within us but are typically untapped. This intelligence is often identified as the unconscious or subconscious mind. Dreams are essentially experiences created through the interactions of the unconscious, subconscious, and conscious mind.

Dreams can grant us a more direct experience with the divine, our guides, ancestors, and nonordinary realms. They can serve as a connection with the spirit world, and often with something even wiser than the human soul. Shamanic dreamwork can be a way to encounter the divine in many forms, receive guidance for developing and deepening awareness, heal ourselves, and find or create meaning for our path. This is particularly true when it comes to change, the paths that can be taken, and the likely associations with those paths.

Shamanic dream incubation involves setting an intention to remember the dream and doing a ceremony that honors this intention. Go beyond asking to interact with the divine in your dreams; assume that you will. Personally, I have had instances where I became aware that I was dreaming three different dreams at one time, and I was observing myself becoming aware of this phenomenon. I also realized that divine intelligence wanted me to realize that I have layers of different dreams and remember my multidimensional awareness.

Dream incubation can be as simple as stating your intention before going to bed, such as counting yourself to sleep and stating: "One, I'm dreaming a dream that is deepening my self-awareness and spiritual growth, and I will remember it in the morning. Two, I'm dreaming a dream that is deepening my self-awareness and spiritual growth and will remember it in the morning. Three, I'm dreaming a dream that is deepening my self-awareness and spiritual growth and will remember it in the morning," and so on. You can also become mindful of your breath or do other breathwork when setting your intention.

A ceremony that honors this intention can involve smudging your bedroom or doing a white fire limpia (refer to pages 81–82), calling in the cardinal spaces around your bed and thanking them for holding sacred space with you while you are sleeping. You can also leave an offering for your divine guides and helpers, asking them to help you in your dreams and deepen your self-awareness and spiritual growth throughout the following day. Other suggestions:

- Get your favorite crystal, hold it in your hands, and program it with love and gratitude, leaving the love vibration as a gift for your divine guides.
- Write a love letter to your divine guides and helpers.
- Get your favorite talisman, kiss it, fill the kiss with love, and leave this offering of love for them.
- Light incense or some resin such as copal for your divine guides and helpers. Fragrance is said to be food for what is etheric in nature.
- Light an oil infuser for them.

You can also use dream plant helpers. Before drinking or eating any of these, ask them to help you choose your ideal question for deepening your self-awareness and spiritual growth, and ask that if you ingest them in the day, you will gracefully remember and understand your dream and its messages. Before going to bed, make a tea with any of the following:

- Jasmine
- Honeysuckle
- Lemon thyme
- Mugwort
- Oregano

You can also eat some:

- Flax seeds
- Caraway seeds
- Bits of onion

During the day, when you drink or eat the plant helper, keep in mind that if you have a déjà vu feeling, this is the universe trying to help you remember, so take note of it.

## Some Methods for Dream Recall

**Waking up.** Wake up slowly and motionlessly. When you awaken from a dream, no matter what time it is, lie still, and try to recall as many details as possible from your dream. Let your eyes stay closed, and put aside any thoughts or worries about the day ahead.

**Collect fragments.** Start with what you do remember. Often memory kicks in from association. If you can't recall anything, try imagining a dream you might have had, and ask yourself, "Did I dream about this?"

**Look to your emotions.** If you have absolutely no recall, turn your focus to how you feel. Are your emotions positive or negative? Have you awakened in a good mood? Try to work backward and discover why you feel the way you do.

**Word association.** Try word association. Focus on the first word that comes to mind to see if this jogs any memories.

**Switch sleeping positions.** If you're still hitting a memory block, switch the position you are lying in. Move slowly to your side, back, stomach: we can often recall the experience when we are lying in the position in which we had the dream.

**Dream journal.** Write down your dreams within 5 minutes of waking up. Experts say that dreams are typically 90 percent forgotten within 10 minutes.

After you remember your dreams, share and talk about them with family, friends, or healing practitioners. Maintain a safe environment where you can talk about your dreams, receive helpful feedback, and support others who are sharing their dreams. If you are flying solo, then some kind of journaling is definitely necessary for understanding and interpreting what came forward in your dreams. You can also use some shamanic dreamwork methods for interpreting your dreams and using your dream journal that are discussed in the next chapter.

### Renee Releases Self-Limiting Beliefs

Sunset energies are ideal for releasing self-limiting beliefs, especially when we couple it with morning rites that affirm self-love. Connecting to the sunset energies, write a list of self-limiting beliefs, thoughts, and statements; then transform each statement into a positive one and make it into a mantra. This will enable you to release and rewire yourself toward a healthy and loving self-perception.

When Renee came to see me, she had a negative and debilitating self-image. According to her, she did not follow through with anything and did not feel good about herself personally. She was a wife and stay-at-home mother of two children, who were now adults and in school. She experienced waves of crying spells, depression, and sadness and did not feel motivated to do anything for her own benefit. She also had health concerns that often left her unable to walk without serious pain, among other matters that the doctors could not explain.

When Renee first came to see me, I recommended that she start her day by connecting to the morning sun for rejuvenation and that she do something for herself that reflected self-love and self-care. For a month, she did just that.

I saw her a month later, and this time she was radiating. She was engaging in daily morning practices of self-love with meditations and walks. She was also superexcited because she had just had an appointment with a surgeon who told her that he could help her release the debilitating pain in her leg, although she would have to undergo a series of surgeries. I knew from my personal experience that positive mental and emotional states are essential to the recovery process.

I recommended that Renee now connect with the sunset and reflect on limiting beliefs she was ready to release. Then she was to do the journaling exercise and replace those limitations with positive, self-affirming ones and make them into mantras. There was a little hiccup a week later, when the surgeon told her that he was unsure whether the surgeries were going to be successful on account of a recent MRI. But I told her these positive mantras were going to be her lifeline.

Renee continued with her discipline of self-love by stating these positive mantras, but she was unsure that this was enough. I assured her that it was more than enough. She had to be patient, compassionate, and loving with herself during her series of surgeries. And she was.

Months later, after working with the morning and sunset energies, she is full of life and incredibly positive about her health. Her self-image and self-esteem have also dramatically improved. We are now in the process of engaging in shamanic dreamwork to develop her spiritual awareness, faith, and love for life.

# 6

# Midnight and Predawn

## *Intersections with Nonordinary Realms*

For both the ancient Mexica and Maya, night, especially late night—midnight and predawn—was when the veils of reality became thinner. It was a mythic time when divine supernatural beings and demons intersected with the mundane world and appeared to people in dreams, nature, and temples.[1] Night was associated with the Underworld and transformation, because, as we have seen, the sun deity journeyed into the Underworld, died nine times, and was transformed into a jaguar, a Lord of the Night.[2] These connections made it likely that the people would also converge with the Underworld late at night. The tests, trials, and tribulations of the Underworld (and by extension nighttime) required humility and discipline, which were typically expressed with diligent ritual offerings.[3]

Next to sunset, midnight was one of the most important times for observing celestial happenings; prognosticating probable outcomes; and performing rituals to ensure prosperity and abundance. Temple shamans also engaged in ritual offerings, and performed limpias on themselves at the *temazcales* (sweat baths) to cleanse themselves and make themselves more capable of traveling into nonordinary realms and conversing with supernatural beings and ancestors there.

Predawn, going from three o'clock in the morning until dawn, was also an important ritual period.[4] The energies of this period were uncertain yet transformative. Possibly dangerous energies were averted with devout offerings, humility, and invoking divine aid. This period also marked a time of shamanic dreamwork and dream interpretation. Shamanic dreamwork was particularly important, as dreams were seen as being divinatory in nature and provided guidance. In dreams, people could leave their bodies through their tonalli and journey into the nonordinary realms.[5] Skilled shamans were also known to enter other people's dreams to see into a situation, cause death or illnesses, obtain cures, determine one's animal coessence or spirit guide, or seek divine guidance.[6]

## MIDNIGHT

*Fantastic, Mythical, and Transformative*

Midnight marked a transformative time, a reference point for new cycles of celestial events and different calendrical periods. The Mexica believed that midnight was also one of the most significant points of reference in determining whether the world would persevere for another fifty-two years in the New Fire Ceremony, Xiuhmolpilli, "binding of the years," that marked a complete cycle of the Calendar Round. They thought the world they lived in would come to an end at one of these fifty-two-year periods. On the night of this rite, all the shamans of Templo Mayor left during the first quarter of the night and made their way to the summit of the mountain Uixachtecatl. All the fires in the entire Aztec empire were extinguished, including those in the temples and homes.

The shamans reached the summit at midnight, where a great pyramid stood. They waited until they saw the Pleiades at their zenith. If the Pleiades moved beyond their zenith, they knew the heavens and sun would continue to move and they would have another fifty-two years. Once they saw movement, they lit a New Fire, which signaled the continuation of the world as well as a new cycle.[7]

The Mexica also had a fire limpia, a New Fire at midnight in honor of their fire deity Xiuhtecutli on the tenth day of the eighteenth month, Izcalli ("sprout," "growth," or "rebirth"), and pleaded to him to help their plants and children grow.[8] They adorned an image of Xiuhtecutli with a brilliant mask made of a green stone horizontally striped with turquoise. They placed a quetzal feather crown on his head and dressed him in a gleaming cape of quetzal feathers. They placed a brazier before him and made offerings of copal. At midnight, the shaman made a New Fire in his honor and pleaded with him. At dawn, the people came forward and placed tamales stuffed with greens before the image, or laid them as offerings in their homes.[9] The New Fire at midnight ensured the new harvest of the next season's coming crops.

Prior to midnight, trumpets were sounded throughout the Aztec empire to wake people and let them know that midnight was coming, an important time for offerings.[10] Water limpias in the form of sweat baths were performed nightly at midnight by the fire shamans, as an offering and to cleanse themselves.[11] The elders of each district also held sweat baths at midnight on the fifth day of the fifteenth month, Panquetzaliztli, as an offering and to cleanse themselves.[12] At midnight, the youths who served in the temple of Huitzilopochtli brought the wood that was to be burned, arranged the branches, adorned the temple, once again blew the trumpets to awaken the people so they too could make offerings, and engaged in the tlenemactli incense ceremony.[13]

Midnight was also the time of the Teotleco feast when the shamans expected to see the mark of Huitzilopochtli on the tub full of corn dough they had left in front of his image at dusk. At midnight they approached the tub with their torches to look for the footprint, which indicated that he would come to be born on Earth and that the old gods would arrive on Earth the next day. When they saw the mark, they sounded the trumpets, and a great shout went out, announcing the arrival and birth of the warrior.[14] As soon as they heard the instruments, people went to offer food at the temples and shrines.[15]

## PREDAWN

*Precarious and Insightful*

The time from approximately 3 a.m. until dawn marked a precarious period, as the sun was undergoing its last trials through the Underworld. To avert danger and ensure the many gifts that came with dawn, it was believed necessary to engage in diligent predawn offerings.

A very important deity that was revered at this time was Venus as the Morning Star, who was greatly feared during the dry seasons, but who also had benevolent aspects.[16] In the Maya Postclassic Dresden Codex, there are five distinct Morning Star deities, or aspects of the same deity. Even though the five gods are shown in identical poses, they represent five different seasonal aspects of Venus, spanning the rainy and dry seasons, and are associated with different Calendar Round dates, recording an eight-year period that traces five heliacal rise dates, from 1221 to 1227 CE.[17] They all wear war regalia, darts, and shields and have dead victims just below their pictures, signaling that these deities were dangerous.[18] It appears that the Morning Star deity was most dangerous during the dry season. The second seasonal manifestation of the Morning Star was Lahun Chan (10 Sky), whose headdress has a prominent maize element like that of the corn god. This manifestation probably coincided with the rainy season and possibly represented a more benevolent Morning Star, as corn generally had positive connotations.[19]

For the Mexica, people believed that when the Morning Star first emerged after not being present in the sky, the rays of the Morning Star could be dangerous and cause sickness and misfortunes. The emerging Morning Star took place on the sixteenth month, Atemoztli (descent of the water), which coincided with the dry season and warfare.[20] The people of the Aztec empire stayed in their homes and blocked all outlets and openings in their homes to prevent the rays of the Morning Star from emanating into their homes.[21] The Venus Morning Star god, Tlahuizcalpantecuhtli, seems to have been associated with this dry season in the Codex Borgia.[22] He is often depicted with a skeletal head or headdress, wearing prominent flint darts in his headband, holding weaponry, and adorned with star signs on his body.[23] Sahagún points out that the rays of the Morning Star could also be benevolent.[24] This was likely during a fortuitous rainy season, and when they were able to appease this deity with diligent offerings.

Ritual offerings at predawn took many forms, including water limpias, food offerings, *barridas* (sweeping as a shamanic cleanse), incense offerings, and invocations. Even children and elders were expected to take part in these rites. On the twelfth month, at the end of the Pachtontli festivities, all the people were expected to go to the river before dawn and cleanse themselves in the water from improprieties and transgressions. Failure to do so could result in ills and contagious diseases. These water limpias continued through dawn.[25]

Noble daughters and sons were taught to wake every day before dawn, offer incense and food, sweep, and say their invocations to the deities.[26] Fathers and mothers woke up their young unmarried women to make offerings of flowers, chia, corn, and little tortillas and leave them before the gods' images.[27] Children were also required to sweep and raise a ladle smoking of copal to the four cardinal directions as offerings to their deities.[28]

The predawn period also marked the time and space of dreams. Sahagún notes that the people went to bed at 10 p.m. This means that the people were likely experiencing their "active phase" of sleeping, when we tend to dream more and for longer periods, during predawn.[29] There are two distinct phases of sleep: a quiet phase and an active phase, which are distinguished by changes in brain waves, eye movements, and muscle tone. The quiet phase is a state of restful inactivity, when mental activity is low, the metabolic rate is at a minimum, and growth hormones are released, facilitating restorative processes.[30] In the active phase, also known as the rapid eye movement (REM) phase, the eyes move rapidly, breathing becomes quick and irregular, the brain burns as much fuel as it does in the waking state, and longer and more vivid dreams tend to occur. The length of the REM periods increases, and the intervals between these periods decrease as night proceeds, which means that the first dream of the night is the shortest, perhaps only ten minutes. After six to seven hours of sleep, dream periods can be forty-five minutes or longer. We thus tend to dream more in the later part of the night.[31]

Sahagún noted in his *Primeros Memoriales* that the shamans who performed dream interpretation were also those who interpreted the auguries of the lunar divinatory calendar, the tonalpohualli. They were known as *tonalpouhque*.[32] The tonalpouhque diagnosed illnesses, determined commitments and vows to be made to deities, and predicted whether someone would soon die and his or her cause of death, among other important matters.[33]

## RECOMMENDED RITES

### Midnight and Predawn

## WORKING WITH THE ENERGIES OF MIDNIGHT

For the ancient Mexica and Maya, midnight was a time when the veils between the ordinary and nonordinary realms were thin. People and shamans tapped into these realms through dreams and ceremonies. Along with its phantasmic nature, midnight signified a time of transformation, marking a reference point for new cycles of celestial events and different calendrical periods.

Following is a list of sacred activities and a night sun deity that can be used to access the energies of midnight.

- Purging and cleansing rites
- Shamanic dreamwork, lucid dreaming, and dream interpretation
- Receiving divine guidance
- Strengthening connections with guides or ancestors
- Ritual offerings
- Transitional ceremonies; changing outcomes
- Rites of healing and divination
- Night Sun Deity, Yohualtecuhtli (Lord of the Night)*

You can work with the energies of midnight from slightly before midnight up to 2 a.m., or at any time of the day by opening your heart and tapping into this period with your pure intention to do so. Generally, however, the rites tend to be much more potent if we can work at the actual time.

## *Shamanic Breathwork for Purging Bad Habits*

Take a moment to connect to the serene, peaceful, and transformative night sun and sky. Thank the night sky, the night sun, and moon for helping you to purge bad habits. Next, engage in the following breathwork rites.

### Maya Coming to the Surface Mudra

Make a gentle fist with both hands, and have the thumb over the middle digit of the index and middle fingers. Place both hands against and between the navel and sternum on the solar plexus. This acupressure point stimulates the solar plexus. Inhale, and exhale with an "OH." Repeat 3 times.

### Purging Breathwork

This breathwork practice induces trance states and helps to release toxins from the body.

*The wise older sun, which was often illustrated with yellow face paint, a red semicircle as a ridge embracing his eye when depicted from the side, fangs, and a spiny zoomorphic body with his face coming out of a crocodile's mouth and holding a sweeping device as well as flint knives.

Get comfortable, sit in an upright position, and close your eyes. Take 8 deep and slow inhales into the nose and exhales out of the mouth. Make sure that there are no gaps between the inhale and exhale, so that the breath is continuous.

Now take another 9 inhales into the nose and out of the mouth, going a little faster, but ensure that your body does not tense up. Again, do not pause between the inhale and the exhale, so that the breath is continuous.

After these 9 inhales and exhales, take another 10 inhales into the nose and exhales out of the mouth, a little faster, but not so fast as to tense up the body. Again, do not pause between the inhale and the exhale.

Now take another 9 inhales into the nose and exhales out of the mouth, but slow it down, again keeping the breath continuous.

Finally, return to the long and deep inhales, 8 into the nose and out of the mouth.

Repeat these cycles until you feel you have entered into a slight meditative state.

## Connecting to the Midnight Sun

Focus on your breath, letting it bring you into a soft trance state. Set the intention to journey into the realm of midnight and the space of positive transformation through your sacred heart.

See yourself immersed in the violet fires, throwing fear, doubt, and toxic emotions into them. Then see yourself enveloped in the white fires of purification and resurrection, allowing them to purify you further and open you up to your full potential. (For more information on traveling into and out of the sacred heart, review pages 71–72.)

Allow yourself to go into a deeper trance state, and ask yourself what habits you would like to purge. Let grandfather night sun pour his wisdom onto you, and receive his energies, giving you the discipline to change and be good and loving to yourself.

Thank grandfather sun for helping you to facilitate change in the ideal way. If you have time, ask if there is anything you need to know about the change or any steps you need to take.

Breathe into these last questions, and thank the night sun and the other divine forces that resonate with you for helping you understand and for giving you the strength to change, accept the unchangeable, and remove yourself from the unacceptable.

When you feel complete, go out through your sacred heart, seeing yourself immersed once again in the sacred white fires of purification and resurrection, and then in the violet fires. Take 6 deep inhales through the nose and exhales out of the mouth. Now allow some time to reflect on what you saw, heard, felt, or learned. Thank the midnight sun for guiding and helping you.

## *Ritual Offerings: Coming Full Circle to Strengthen an Intention*

For this rite you will need:

- An offering (see below)
- Parchment paper
- A No. 2 pencil
- An oil or perfume
- A picture of yourself

Start this rite at night, preferably close to midnight and on a full moon. Place your favorite scent, an oil or perfume, on the parchment paper, on your picture, and on you. Allow yourself to go into a light meditative trance state by listening to repetitive deep drumbeats, doing any one of the recommended shamanic breathwork practices, or by simply setting the intention. Connect with the midnight sun and the moon by sending love and gratitude to them.

From this space of love and gratitude, write down on the paper what you would love to come full circle in manifesting. This is related to something you have already been working toward in some way, whether it be through another rite, taking some other action (like going on a job interview and setting the intention to obtain an ideal job), or doing dreamwork around this intention. You are setting the intention that you are ready for it to come to fruition.

After you have written down your intention, choose your offerings. Copal is always ideal. Other offerings that the night sun and moon love include feathers, cacao, tobacco, corn, fruit platters, cinnamon sticks, flowers, earth, water, fire as a burning candle, an idol image or statute or other sacred item. Here is a little more about the items:

**Cornmeal or corncobs** invite the wisdom of our ancestors and deepen our spiritual connection to them.

**Cacao** ensures great fortune and prosperity.

**Cinnamon sticks** invite success and strengthen the power to change anything.

**Earth** is a life-giving force and helps to make intentions fertile.

**Water** promotes divinatory gifts and emotional resilience.

**Flowers** welcome in abundance, joy, and great fortune.

**Tobacco** invites in the wisdom of our ancestors and deepens our spiritual connection to them, as well as healing and purifying.

**Feathers** promote divinatory and intuitive work.

Offer the offering to the midnight sun and to the moon, if you are working with the moon. Thank them for helping you to manifest your intention. Place the offering next to your petition and picture.

Do this every night for 4 (4 is associated with stability) nights with the same or different offerings. You can make this ritual as elaborate or simple as you like. Place your favorite scent on you, your picture, and your petition every night for 4 nights. Make sure the scent is still on you before going to bed. Every night, connect with and thank the midnight sun and moon for helping your intention to manifest with impeccability.

Then leave the picture or paper on your altar or somewhere special. When your intention comes to be, bury the picture and paper in the Earth.

## MORE ELABORATE MIDNIGHT RITES

### *Tarot:* La Cruz *(The Cross)*

For this rite you will need the following items:

- Your favorite Tarot deck
- Any or all of these flowers or herbs (must be dry): parsley, St. John's wort, yarrow leaves or flowers, dried daisies, or dried helichrysum. All of these facilitate accurate divinatory work.
- Charcoal tablet
- Glazed brazier
- Wooden stick matches
- Florida water* or access to running water.

I recommend doing this rite at nighttime, preferably at midnight. While divination is great to do in the morning, it lends itself more to creating or bringing something into being as we intuit a situation. Nighttime, on the other hand, is ideal for doing divination in areas where we simply need guidance, because the veils of reality are thin at this time, and we have access to the normally unseen.

Connect with the midnight sun, and thank it for helping you to transcend time and space and see into a situation. Cleanse your hands with Florida water, or place your hands under running water and thank the water for cleansing your hands. Light the charcoal tablet with a match, and place it on the brazier. Put the herbs or flowers on the charcoal, and thank their spirit essence for enabling you to see into a situation.

Shuffle the cards facing down, while asking your question. Thank your cards for answering your question in divine perfection. Lay the cards out in a flat line, facing down, in this manner:

---

*Florida water is a cleansing liquid that contains alcohol as its base, spring or blessed water, and aromatic cleansing flowers and herbs. You can buy Florida water at pharmacies that have an ethnic section, or make it from scratch.

- The first card goes in the center. It is the theme of your question.
- The second card goes to the left. It is a gift that you are unaware of but is there to aid you.
- The third card goes to the right. It is a gift you are aware of but have not been using, although it is there to aid you.
- The fourth card goes at the bottom. This is the energy of the path concerning the question.
- Fifth card goes at the top. This card is what the end result will look like.

As you turn up the cards in this order, pay attention to your breath, inhaling and exhaling slowly. If you know what the cards mean immediately, perfect. If not, tune into the different meanings and feel into the one from which you feel an energy surge; this is the right one. Afterward, thank the herbs, flowers, cards, and night sun for helping you.

## WORKING WITH THE ENERGIES OF PREDAWN

The ancient Mexica and Maya regarded the energies of predawn as uncertain, possibly dangerous, but capable of providing incredible insights. Because these energies were highly liminal and ambiguous, diligent offerings were performed at this time. Shamanic dreamwork was also practiced, although the dream sharing and interpretation likely took place after predawn.

The following is a list of sacred items, activities, and a night sun deity associated with predawn:

- Ritual offerings and prayers
- Practices inspiring humility and grace (also performed before going to bed)
- Shamanic dreamwork, lucid dreaming, and dream interpretation
- Strengthening connections with our guides or ancestors
- Receiving divine guidance

- Rites to shift and influence circumstances
- Yohualtecuhtli (Lord of the Night)*

### *Enhancing Prophetic Dreams and Strengthening Connection with Guides and Ancestors*

If you happen to wake up at three o'clock in the morning, incubate your dreams with an intention and offering. Review the methods on how to incubate your dreams on pages 100–103, but this time set the intention of having a prophetic dream or strengthening your connection to your guides and ancestors. Use any of the following offerings to enhance prophetic dreams:

- Burn caraway seeds on a charcoal tablet, and leave some out as an offering. The ones that are left as an offering can be placed back into the Earth or on your altar when you wake up.
- Place a little jasmine oil between your upper lip and nose, and leave the bottle open on your nightstand or next to your bed.
- Eat a little oregano, and put a few leaves out as an offering. You can place them back into the Earth or on your altar when you wake up.
- Burn dry rosemary on a charcoal tablet, and leave some out as an offering. The rosemary that is left as an offering can be placed back into the Earth or on your altar when you wake up.

Have your offering ready before going to bed so you can do this predawn rite gracefully and easily go back to bed.

## MORE ELABORATE PREDAWN RITES

### *Creating a Prophetic Dream Tincture*

If you can purchase bobinsana leaves online, or obtain them elsewhere, they are ideal for this tincture. Along with facilitating prophetic dreams,

*See footnote on page 112 for more on Yohualtecuhtli.

bobinsana is known to heal our dreams and the unconscious mind. It can open and heal the heart; increase empathy, clarity, and concentration; and provide spiritual grounding. It is also used as a heart tonic, stimulant, and energizer. Working with bobinsana solely as a tincture is highly recommended, at least initially.

You can also make another prophetic dream tincture with any of the following plants (dry or fresh) and seeds: jasmine, caraway seeds, oregano, rosemary, honeysuckle, lemon thyme, and flax seeds.

You will need a clean amber bottle that has a tight lid, a clean glass, a label for your bottle, and cheesecloth.

The most potent tinctures are made with pure cane alcohol. But this is illegal in many places, so gin or vodka can be substituted. Nonalcoholic tinctures can be made with vegetable glycerine or apple cider vinegar, but they are usually not as effective in drawing out all of the plant's medicinal qualities. Nevertheless, they are a good choice if you want to avoid alcohol. Plant properties are generally dissolved more easily in alcohol, which draws out the medicinal qualities of the plant, including alkaloids, volatile oils, and resins. Alcohol-based tinctures can also last for several years and are a convenient way to preserve medicinal herbs.

Steps:

- Chop the plants very fine, or crush the seeds with a mortar and pestle, and place them in a clean jar. Fill the bottle about 75 percent full with the seeds or plants.
- Fill the bottle almost to the top with alcohol. The plants and seeds will expand, so you want to leave a little bit of space.
- Close the bottle with a tight lid.
- Label your bottle, indicating the ingredients and the date.
- Allow the mixture to steep for at least 2 to 6 weeks in a cool, dark place.
- Shake the bottle daily.
- On the last day, don't shake the bottle. Allow the herbs to settle.
- Pour the tincture through a cheesecloth-lined strainer into a clean glass.

- Place the plants and seeds that were in the bottle in a compost bin or back in the Earth.
- Clean the bottle, and pour the tincture into it.

Connect with the predawn sun and the spirit essence of the plants of your tincture to ensure that you will have prophetic dreams and remember them. You can use the tincture directly from the bottle with a euro dropper. Place 4 drops of the tincture under your tongue before going to bed. (Refer to page 103 for dream recall methods.)

## *Fourteen-Day Rite to Change Outcomes*

For this rite you will need:

- A large vase that can fit 7 regular-size apples
- Seven green apples
- Seven red apples
- Seven quarters
- Parchment paper
- A No. 2 pencil
- Two charcoal tablets
- Copal
- Wooden stick matches
- Glazed brazier
- A picture of you

Do this rite after nightfall, or preferably just before dawn. Connect with the predawn sun, and thank the night sun for transforming a situation for you. Write down what you would like to change in your life on the paper. Place the petition, your picture, and the 7 quarters at the bottom of the vase, and then put the 7 green apples in the vase.

Light a charcoal tablet, and place copal on it next to the vase. This cleanses the space and also acts as an offering. Leave the contents of the vase intact for 7 full days.

Plate 1. Image of Tonatiuh with sun insignia.

*From Codex Borgia, Joseph Florimond, duc de Loubat Collection (Loubat 1898), page 18. Courtesy of Ancient Americas at LACMA.*

*Note to the Reader:* Plates 3, 7, 8, 9, and 10 have been rotated 90 degrees counterclockwise so they can be read from top to bottom, as intended. These images come from the Codex Borgia and appear horizontal in the original text.

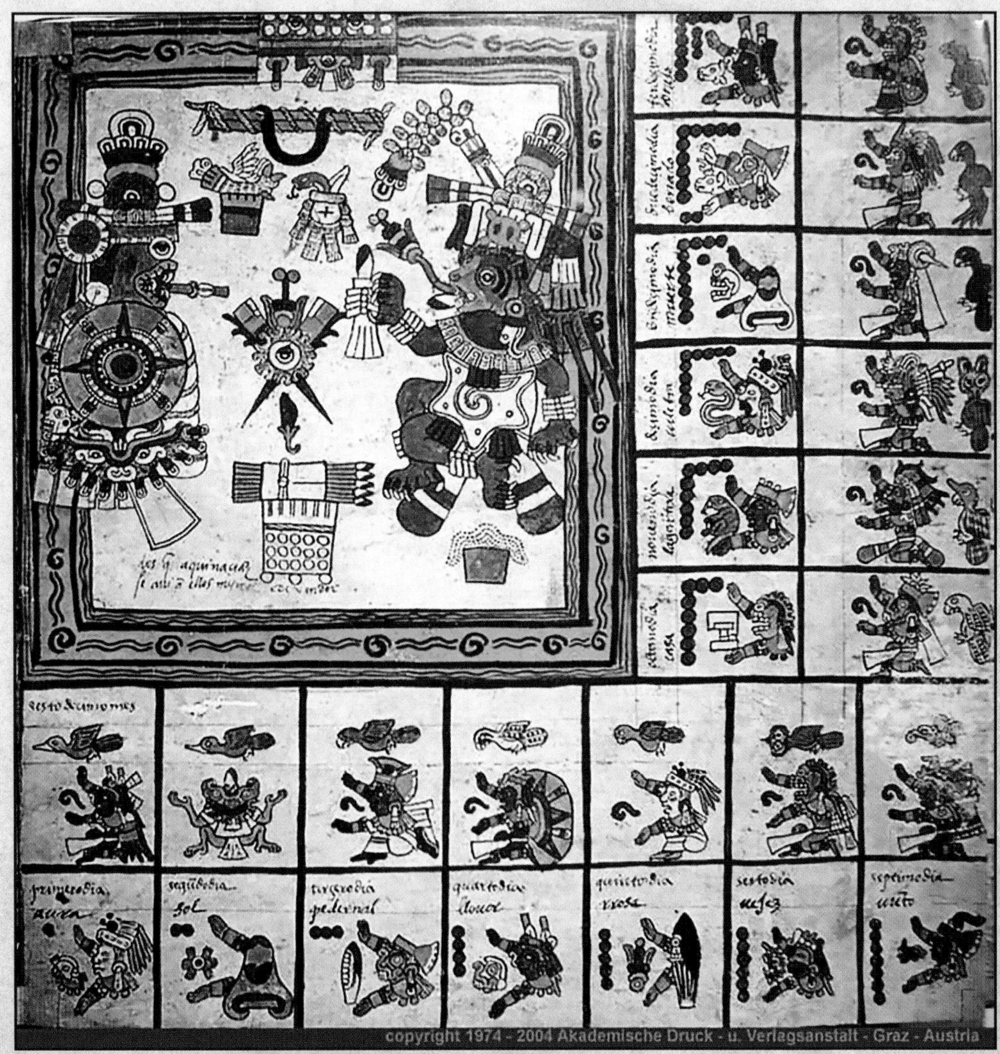


Plate 2. Xolotl facing Tlalchitonatiuh, who is displayed in a mortuary bundle with a sun insignia.

*From Codex Borbonicus, Joseph Florimond, duc de Loubat Collection (Loubat 1899), page 16. Courtesy of Ancient Americas at LACMA.*

Plate 3. Xochipilli at the summer solstice.

*From Codex Borgia, Joseph Florimond, duc de Loubat Collection (Loubat 1898), page 37. Courtesy of Ancient Americas at LACMA.*

Plate 4 (below left). Aged Deity I weaving.

*From Madrid Codex, Brasseur de Bourbourg and Léon de Rosny, page 102c. Courtesy of Ancient Americas at LACMA.*

Plate 5 (below right). Aged Deity I with offerings.

*From Madrid Codex, Brasseur de Bourbourg and Léon de Rosny, page 107b. Courtesy of Ancient Americas at LACMA.*

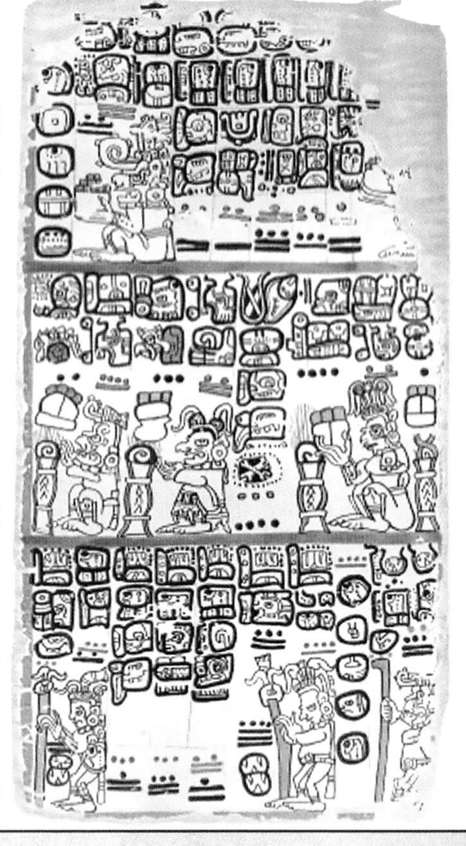

Plate 6. Deity O with inverted jar and falling water.

*From Madrid Codex, Brasseur de Bourbourg and Léon de Rosny, page 10b. Courtesy of Ancient Americas at LACMA.*

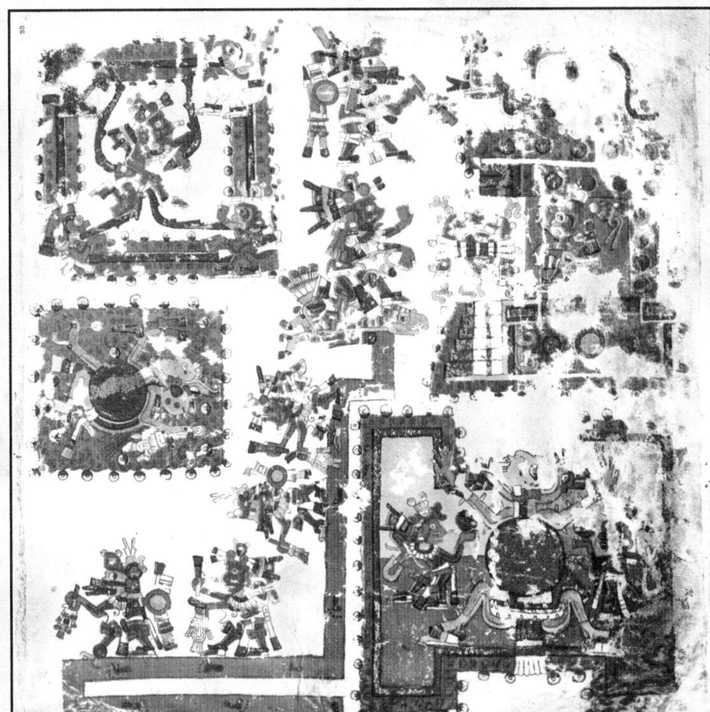

Plate 7. Yohualtecuhtli as an elderly man.

*From Codex Borgia, Joseph Florimond, duc de Loubat Collection (Loubat 1898), page 35. Courtesy of Ancient Americas at LACMA.*

Plate 8. Stripe Eye and Xochipilli carrying an olla or drum and a long trumpet.

*From Codex Borgia, Joseph Florimond, duc de Loubat Collection Loubat 1898), page 39. Courtesy of Ancient Americas at LACMA.*

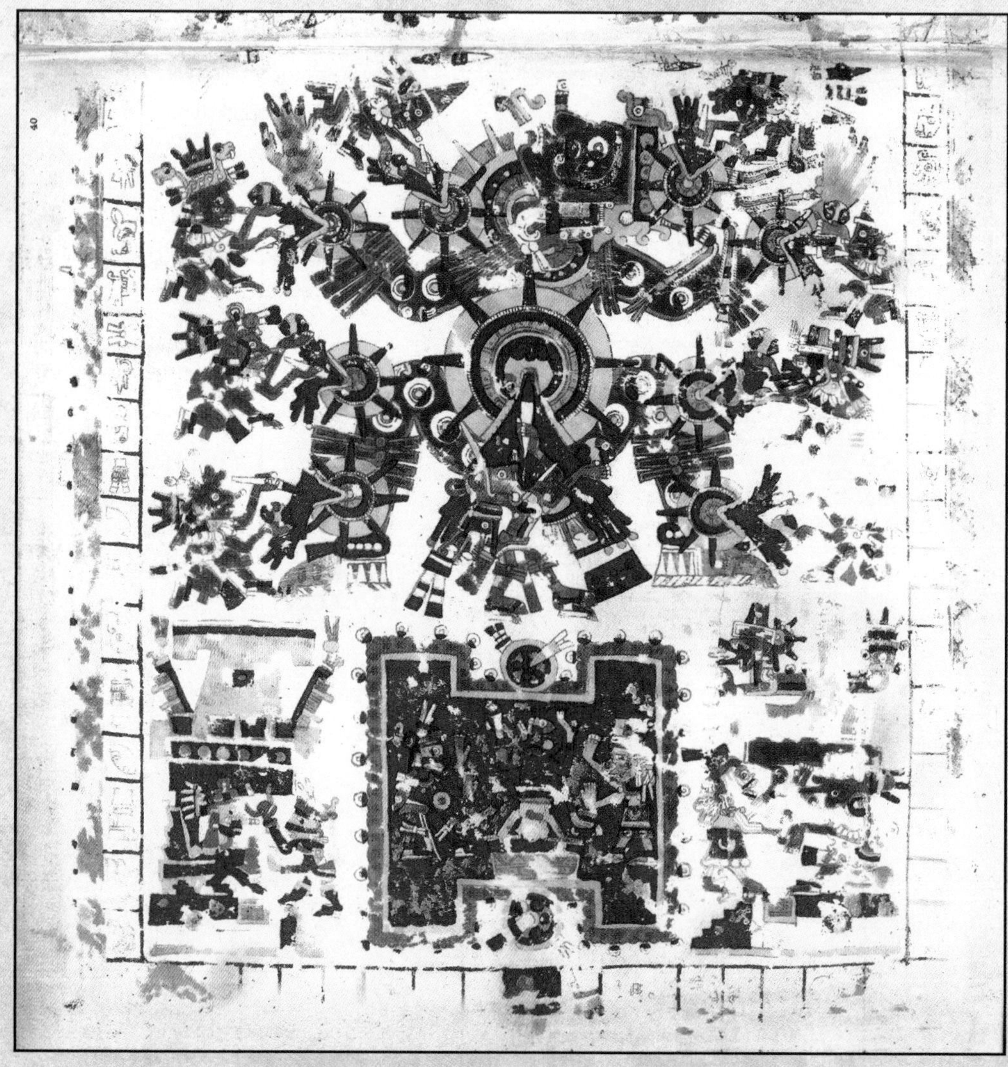

Plate 9. The sun in a birth-giving pose with spots and bumps on the hands and feet identifying him as Nanahuatzin.

*From Codex Borgia, Joseph Florimond, duc de Loubat Collection (Loubat 1898), page 40. Courtesy of Ancient Americas at LACMA.*

Plate 10. Xochiquetzal giving birth to a flowering tree.

*From Codex Borgia, Joseph Florimond, duc de Loubat Collection (Loubat 1898), page 44. Courtesy of Ancient Americas at LACMA.*

Plate 11. Deity O with thirteen inscribed on the deity's chest.

*From Madrid Codex, Brasseur de Bourbourg and Léon de Rosny, page 32b. Courtesy of Ancient Americas at LACMA.*

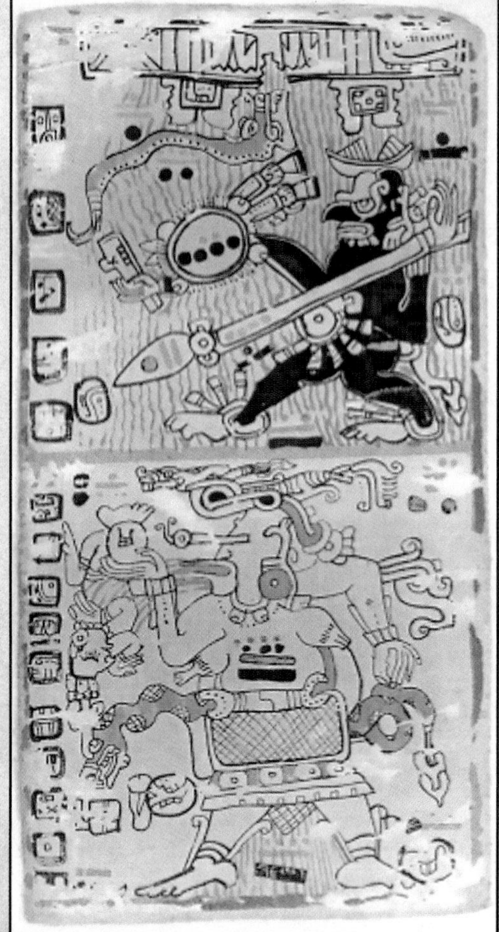

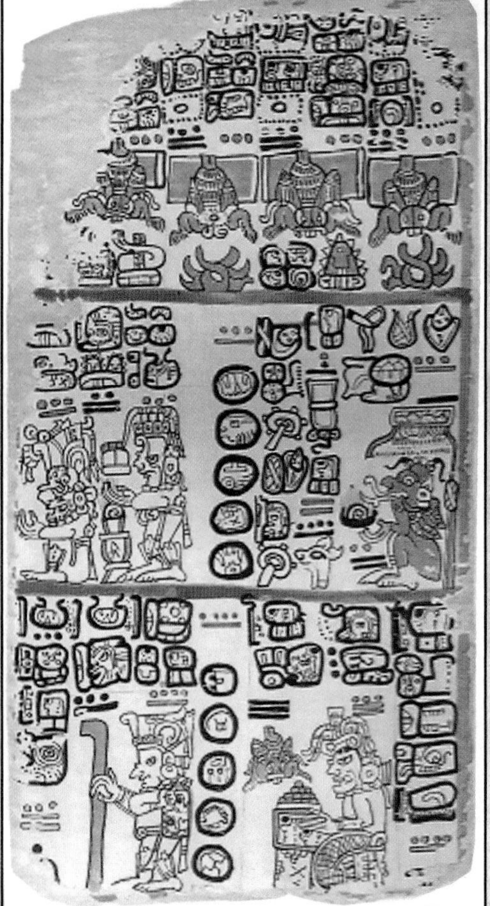

Plate 12. Aged Deity I as the waning moon.

*From Madrid Codex, Brasseur de Bourbourg and Léon de Rosny, page 102c. Courtesy of Ancient Americas at LACMA.*

After the seventh day, remove the green apples and replace them with red apples. Bury the green apples. Do not place them in a compost bin, because they are now carrying the energy of what is being transmuted. Let the Earth and sun transmute this energy for you.

After placing the red apples in the vase, light another charcoal tablet, and place copal on it. Let the contents of the vase remain intact for 7 days. After the seventh day, bury the red apples. Place the parchment paper and quarters on your altar, or somewhere special. Once the change has occurred, spend the 7 quarters, and bury the parchment paper and picture in the Earth.

---

### Jenny Was Guided to Meet Her Love in a Dream

When Jenny first reached out to me, she wrote an email containing a laundry list of things she wanted to change in her life. Three times she mentioned wanting to meet her partner. The person who had referred her to me was now engaged and was beginning to live a happy, abundant life. This person attested that I had helped them to release that which no longer served them and to shift their consciousness to attract financial prosperity and ideal love.

When Jenny first came to me, as usual, I opened up by encouraging her to share with me whatever she wanted to focus on. She mentioned love last and indicated that her career was of utmost importance. She worked at an advertising agency. Although she was in a job and firm she loved, she had a tyrannical boss. The boss felt threatened by Jenny, who was incredibly sharp, beautiful, and motivated. In the past year, Jenny was able to secure the firm's largest new clients. Her boss, however, was making Jenny's life at work difficult in every way she could, including demeaning and criticizing her work. The boss purposefully gave her last-minute assignments, forcing her to work weekends, and tried to have her work on accounts that were not as prestigious. Jenny was having problems with her digestion, experiencing mild insomnia, and having anxiety issues, especially when her boss belittled her. These health issues began a couple of months after working with her boss.

As homework to change her circumstances, I had Jenny do the fourteen-day rite with apples. After the eighth day, I received a frantic email from Jenny. Apparently her boss had been sick for three days with a stomach flu. She told me that she was concerned. Although she did not care for her boss, she also did not intend to cause her harm. I asked her to confirm her petition and that she had asked for an ideal outcome. She confirmed. I told her not to worry. Her boss's stomach flu was not caused by Jenny.

When Jenny returned to see me the next month, she told me that her boss had been out for an entire week and was working from home on the last couple of days. When her boss came back, she was different, more passive. She began to leave Jenny alone and simply allowed her to do her work.

In the next session, Jenny confided in me that she really wanted a family, but she was in her midthirties and was not in a romantic relationship; she had not been even been out on a date for almost a year. Perplexed, I asked her what she was doing to meet people. She told me that she was doing nothing at present. She had tried online dating apps but hated them. She felt they were incredibly time-consuming and ended up being a waste of time. I recommended that she engage in activities that she enjoyed, but that she go by herself and not with her friends. She said she would consider going hiking to put herself out there, but she would not under any circumstances ever do online dating again.

Jenny came in to see me the following month. While her health was improving, she wanted to focus on her job again. She was working on an advertisement for a new account she had secured, but she was feeling blocked creatively. She had not taken any steps to meet new people and had not engaged in any activities on her own, besides grocery shopping.

I advised her that one of the most effective ways to clear creativity blocks was by engaging in shamanic dreamwork. I told her about the bobinsana tincture, and she asked if I happened to have some already made that she could purchase. I did. Most importantly, I had her engage in dream incubation and intend to receive divine inspiration for her current job assignment. I advised her to engage in diligent nightly rituals with copal next to an offering altar with a petition for ideal divine inspiration, her picture, the company logo of her new client, and a plate containing cacao, flowers, and honey.

I saw Jenny approximately six weeks after that. She had come in for help with dream interpretation and was excited to share that the new account was going astonishingly well. Better yet, there was word that her boss was probably getting promoted and transferred to their San Francisco office. Jenny was elated. She had also gone on two group hiking events on her own. While she had not met anyone she was interested in, she had a great time and felt a regained sense of freedom that she had not been aware was missing.

Jenny also told me about reoccurring dreams she was having involving a friend she had known since high school, although they eventually had grown apart. Her friend was now an attorney and was married. Jenny admitted that she did not go to her friend's wedding. She felt horrible about this, but she told me that life and work had gotten in the way. Jenny did not seem to be willing to talk about why they had grown apart, so I did not press her on these issues.

It was clear from everything Jenny was saying about her dreams that her unconscious dream mind was telling her to contact this friend. I told Jenny that she had to put aside their differences and contact her. We looked her up on Facebook and found her. Jenny messaged her.

At our next session, Jenny came in radiating. She had reached out to her friend, who happened to be having a housewarming party for their new house and invited Jenny. Jenny went and had a great time, and this is where she met Tom. Tom and Jenny instantly became inseparable. They had been together every weekend.

Jenny admitted to me that she saw herself falling in love with him. She asked me what I thought. I told her to move forward with an open heart and mind, and to allow him to prove himself to her before she gave her heart away.

Approximately six months later, they moved in together, and they are deeply in love. Tom comes in to see me, and they definitely have a healthy and loving relationship. Jenny's boss was transferred to the San Francisco office, and Jenny now works with someone else, who trusts and is grateful for Jenny's keen expertise and vision.

---

# 7

# Rites for Lunar Phases

## *New, Waxing, Full, and Waning Moons*

The moon was important to the ancient Mesoamericans, particularly the Central Mexican indigenous peoples of Xaltocan (probably the Otomis), and many Postclassic Maya of the northeastern part of the Yucatán Peninsula, including the island of Cozumel.[1]

The study of the moon and the glyphic passages associated with it have, however, been largely understudied by scholars.[2] While epigraphers have made tremendous advances in the translating of Maya glyphs over the last few decades, they are still vague about the Lunar Series, which contains a large corpus of lunar notations that have only been studied by a handful of scholars.[3] Fortunately, this has been slowly shifting and will, I hope, continue to do so.

The associations of lunar phases with genders and ages provide a significant window for understanding how the Maya perceived the energies emitted by the lunar phases. As explained in chapter 2, the gendered and anthropomorphic identities of the moon were fluid and complex, reflecting lunar phases, activity, and conjunctions. The noneclipsed new moon was often associated with youth, the birth of rulers, and the designations of heirs.[4] The new moon that resulted in a solar eclipse was usually depicted as an aged, anthropomorphic, third-gendered deity.[5] The waxing moon was typically associated with expansion, licentiousness, and growth.[6] The noneclipsed full moon was generally associated with maturity, completion, accession of rulers, and building dedication rites.[7] A full moon involving a lunar eclipse was often associated with war. Depicted as anthropomorphic, with third-gender characteristics, it was greatly feared.[8] The waning moon was typically depicted as an aged deity, associated with death and decrease.[9]

## NEW MOON

*Youth, Births, and New Beginnings*

When Sahagún discusses the moon of the Mexica in the Florentine Codex, he describes him as Tecuciztecatl, the wealthy deity who, as we have seen, first offered himself as a sacrifice to help the sun rise in the creation story of the sun. But it was the poor yet courageous Nanahuatzin who ended up offering himself first and actually became the sun. Tecuciztecatl, ashamed, then offered himself. When he did so, he became the moon and gleamed brilliantly. To darken Tecuciztecatl's face, one of the gods threw a rabbit at it.[10] Although in Sahagún's description the gender of the moon as a male remains the same, its age changes according to its phases. During the new moon phase, the moon is described as a "small bow, like a bent, straw lip ornament—a small one"; accessories associated with young boys.[11]

The Maya codices and artwork also depicted the new moon deities as youthful and associated the new moon with new beginnings, such as heir designations.[12] The youthful lunar deity, Deity I, has been associated with an Earth aspect of the moon and with the new moon.[13] Youth possessed an intrinsic proximity to the nonordinary realms, where supernatural beings and ancestors resided. Spaces were often imbued with sacred power by placing a burial urn in them containing the body of a very small child alongside precious items such as jade and shells. The ancient Maya often viewed infants, both living and dead, as members of a liminal group having intrinsic sacred worth.[14]

Deity I was associated with Earth, fertility, the birth of corn, and lunar aspects. The image of Deity I on the crescent moon (see figure 7.1 on page 128) depicts the god as a third-gender being with attributes of the corn god and lunar goddess.[15] References to corn included the netted short skirt typically worn by the corn deity and a tonsure on the top of Deity I's head, as well as on the top of the crescent moon, perhaps auguring the birth of corn. Next to the tonsure of corn is an *imix* day sign, which was often associated with white lilies, mirrors, divination, and the Earth.[16] Mirrors served as tools of prognostication and self-reflection, and as a way to connect with supernatural beings and ancestors.[17] Here the moon deity is the diviner. Deity I is also seen in a *chok* mudra (which means "to sprinkle" or "offer," and as a noun refers to a "young person, child"),[18] and there are air volutes or offerings of copal floating into Deity I's nose, signaling the god's acceptance of the offering.

The hieroglyphs in the temples of the Cross Group at Palenque indicate that Kan B'ahlam II, the ruler who commissioned these temples, evoked the energies of principal lunar phases to legitimize his reign, commemorating and engaging in an heir designation rite on a new moon. The Cross Group, as discussed in chapter 1, was designed to express solar and lunar hierophanies commemorating critical imperial rites and was also shrines to the three creator deities of Palenque: GI, GII, and GIII. On the Temple of the Cross, the birth of ruler Kan B'ahlam II is commemorated as 9.10.2.6.6 (May 23, 635 CE; only the Long Count is visible), a new moon night. On the Tablet of the Sun at the Temple of the Sun, the heir designation of Kan B'ahlam II is noted as 9.10.8.9.3, 9 Akbal 6 Xul (June 17, 641 CE), corresponding to a new moon. The Tablet of the Sun then goes back in time to the birth of GIII as being 1.18.5.3.6, 13 Cimi 19 Ceh (October 25, 2360 BCE), also a new moon night. Commemorating the ruler's birth and heir designation on a new moon night indicated that these

Figure 7.1. Deity I as a third-gender being with attributes of the corn god and lunar goddess.

*Drawing 5502 by Linda Schele. Copyright © David Schele. Courtesy of Ancient Americas at LACMA.*

imperial events were blessed by the new moon energies of youth and new beginnings.[19]

For the Mexica, the new moon during a solar eclipse was associated with death and danger; it was depicted as aged or anthropomorphic third-gender deities with death symbolism.[20] The sixteenth-century indigenous chronicler Tezozómoc notes that the tzitzimime, vicious beings that attacked the sun during eclipses, were constellations and planets that suddenly become visible during a solar eclipse.[21] Tzitzimitl, one of the tzitzimime, was an aspect of Cihuacoatl.[22] On page 76r of the Codex Magliabechiano, Cihuacoatl is depicted as a third-gender anthropomorphic deity, with a skeletal body, a flag headdress resembling the one placed on the third-gender deity impersonator at the Tititl rite, a dress, and a penis snake coming out of the dress. The tzitzimime were typically depicted as skeletal female figures wearing skirts with skull-and-crossbone designs.[23]

The Postclassic Maya also depicted the new moon deity during a solar eclipse as a third-gender anthropomorphic being. Page 67a of the Dresden Codex shows the new moon during an eclipse as Deity O, the aged lunar deity.[24] Deity O has the usual aged features—Roman nose, markings on the cheek for wrinkles, an extended jaw, a jaguar-spotted eye, feline claws for hands and feet, an open mouth, and a long feminized skirt. The inverted water jug, water coming out of the jug; jade necklace; and serpent headdress all refer to water symbolism.[25] This symbolism, coupled with her age, which was typically associated with dangerous transitions, may be connecting the advent of the solar eclipse with the coming of a heavy rain.

## WAXING MOON

*Expansion, Increase, and Sexuality*

Sahagún refers to the waxing moon as rounded and filled out, analogous to being pregnant.[26] Milbrath asserts that Xochiquetzal on page 44 of the Codex Borgia seems to symbolize the new moon, as her torso is covered by a sun disk with radiant rays, indicating the conjunction of the moon and the sun (see plate 10).[27]

But Xochiquetzal could also be the waxing moon. As was mentioned in chapter 2, in her feminine aspect she is a young deity associated with passionate love, sexual power, flowers, and physical pleasure, and she presides over pregnancy and childbirth. Inside the enclosure of flints and flowers, she lies on the ground, and at her navel she has a red bulging sun, with a heart in the middle, where a multicolored flowering plant is growing.[28] Xochiquetzal as the waxing moon has been likely impregnated by the sun and appears to be giving birth to multicolored flowers.

Xkik, a maiden of the Underworld in the Popol Vuh who becomes pregnant with the Hero Twins, is also probably to be understood as the waxing moon.[29] Xkik goes to a tree on which the Lords of the Underworld had hung the head of Hun Hunahpu, and which shortly after grew luscious gourds. She reaches out for one. The spittle from the head of Hun Hunahpu impregnates her with the second generation of twins, who go on to defeat the Lords of the Underworld. As the waxing moon, Xkik is depicted with young children and offers various foods essential to sustenance, such as fish and corn. The waxing-moon deity also has a malevolent side, however, and brings certain diseases, largely related to sex. She is lascivious and is depicted with many lovers, apparently because her rapid movement through the sky results in many conjunctions.[30]

## FULL MOON

### *Completion and Maturity*

Sahagún describes the full moon as being complete and mature and as having a little rabbit stretched across his face.[31]

In the Popol Vuh, the Hero Twins were transformed into the sun and moon after successfully defeating the Lords of the Underworld. Mesoamerican scholar Dennis Tedlock interprets Xbalanque as the male image of the full moon, called "little jaguar sun," and says the K'iché' Maya use the term "night sun" to identify the full moon.[32] Xbalanque has completed his journey and defeated the Lords of the Underworld when he becomes the full moon.

The full moon was also depicted as an aged mature deity. This aged deity, as Lunar Deity O, is depicted on page 32b of the Madrid Codex and has a thirteen inscribed on the deity's chest, suggesting a link with a count of lunar months (see plate 11). In colonial Yucatec Maya dictionaries, the number thirteen is linked to a phrase describing the full moon.[33] In this scene, the deity appears to be pouring water from her mouth, exposed waterlily breasts, and genitals. She has a serpent headdress with a figure eight underneath, which is likely the glyph for zac ("white"), referring to the whiteness of the moon.[34] In the context of the scene, her serpent belt refers to the water gushing out of the sky. The Eb day sign in front of her serpent sky belt combines the symbols for death and water to signify destructive water.[35] The net of corn protruding out of her skirt may allude to phallic symbolism, suggesting her third-gender identity and its ties to weather transition, the coming of destructive water and wind.

The full moon rites at Palenque honored cycles of completion and maturity. On July 26, 690, a full moon blessed the Temple of the Sun at Palenque with its energies of completion.[36] Two days before, to prepare for this auspicious event, Kan B'ahlam II had performed a dedication rite for the temple.[37] Temple dedications were limpias, which purified, activated, and renewed their sacred essence energy. This energy could be renewed with specific soul energy signatures, including those of a ruler, embodying the incarnation of a creator deity into the ruler; the cycle of a family dynasty; or some other sacred union. The temples did not simply depict these events; they were alive and embodied them.[38]

The day after the peak of the full moon, Kan B'ahlam II sealed the revivification of the Temple of the Sun with a liquid rich in sacred essence energy—his blood—and engaged in a bloodletting rite. Two days later, the people celebrated the anniversary of the accession of

Kan B'ahlam II's father, K'inich Janaab' Pakal, to the throne.[39] These rites commemorated a cycle of accession by the dynasty and renewed the sacred temple with soul energy of the ruler and his father. As recorded on the Zapata panel of Palenque, the accession of Kan B'ahlam II was performed during a full moon, and interestingly, the ruler's death was recorded one day before a full moon. Two and a half years later, his soul is recorded as rising from the Underworld, likely to join his father in the Upperworld floral paradise.[40] These lunar rites concerning critical stages associated with Kan B'ahlam II—his accession, death, and apotheosis—were recorded as taking place on or a day or two within the full moon, demonstrating that the moon empowered his reign and apotheosis.

Milbrath asserts that the dismemberment of middle-aged Coyolxuahqui by her brother Huitzilopochtli, who is associated with the sun, may be a metaphor for an eclipse of the full moon by the sun.[41] In many of the stories associated with the dismemberment of Coyolxuahqui, Huitzilopochtli confronts her because he believes she is going to kill their mother. He goes to war with her and their four hundred brothers—an analogy to the war and strife that the Maya believed took place at eclipses.

Facing enemies and going to war during a full moon lunar eclipse may also have been something the Maya, or at least the Classic Maya, engaged in. The final date on the Tablet of the Sun at Palenque relates to a war that coincided with a partial lunar eclipse. On that date, Smoking Squirrel of Naranjo and Ah Cacaw of Tikal went to war with the cities of Ucanal and Calakmul respectively.[42]

## WANING MOON

*Dying, Decreasing, and Aging*

According to Sahagún, the waning moon as a male was dying, and when he had completely disappeared, it was said that "the moon hath died."[43] Contemporary Mesoamerican peoples often describe the waning moon in anthropomorphic terms and say it is an old person.[44] In the Popol Vuh, the grandmother of the Hero Twins, Xmucane, has been identified as the waning moon.[45] Xmucane also takes the role of an aged midwife and diviner.[46]

Aged Deity I as the waning moon is depicted as a beekeeper on page 108c of the Madrid Codex. Deity I is wearing a beaded long skirt that goes below the knee, which suggests her femininity (see plate 12).[47] She has the typical aged features: a Roman nose, an open mouth showing one tooth, and markings on the cheek to indicate wrinkles, and even though she is topless, she has no breasts, suggesting she is postmenopausal. Her headdress is shaped as a lazy eight with the glyph zac (white), but the two are separated, probably referring to the whiteness of the decreasing moon. The altar that is holding her honey has Kaban curl images, the phonetic value of "u," the Yucatec Mayan term for "moon."[48] She is harvesting honey, an activity associated with the waning moon by contemporary Maya.[49]

## RECOMMENDED RITES

### New, Waxing, Full, and Waning Moon

## WORKING WITH THE ENERGIES OF THE NEW MOON

For the ancient Mexica and Maya, the new moon was generally understood as being young, emitting energies that fostered new ventures, births, and new cycles. Coupled with the night sun's energies of transformation, engaging in night ceremonies on a new moon can facilitate successful new beginnings.

The new moon of a solar eclipse, however, could be dangerous. Most people today connected with curanderismo traditions are still very discerning during eclipses, especially solar eclipses. While I am not terrified of eclipses by any means and utilize their energies, I use discernment. One simple rite I engage in during these times is to change the glass of water by my front door, which has a black obsidian arrowhead in it, and run the arrowhead under running water to cleanse it. Don Fernando, one of my Yucatec Maya mentors, taught me to do this. If I do have to go out on an eclipse, I always have at least one obsidian arrowhead touching my skin.

I utilize new moon and solar eclipse energies if I want to cloak and camouflage something. To cloak and camouflage something, simply state this in your intention. If I need to cloak something before the next eclipse, I do it during a waning moon phase. Cloaking keeps something unseen, and to camouflage the information means that it does not appear as it is; rather, something else appears in its place. Know that you can tailor this practice according to your needs.

In the next section, I recommend things to consider in wording intentions for mantras, invocations, and petitions. Here are some activities, sacred items, a new moon deity, and a new moon solar eclipse deity that can be used and invoked to access new moon energies:

- Rites to birth a new project
- Fertility rites to ensure impregnation or a successful and healthy birth
- Rites involving seeds
- Water rites: water, as discussed in chapter 2, was often associated with lunar deities, particularly female ones
- Rites for changes to an existing project
- Moonstone: choose the color based on what feels right while reflecting on what you are choosing to manifest*
- Shells are associated with moon and water rites and can hold or convey sacred essence energy[50]
- Sacred items that are new or represent youth, which strengthen links with nonordinary realm
- Charging new sacred tools under a new moon and setting the inten-

*Refer to pages 73–74 to read more about the colors of crystals and their effects.

tion to imprint your signature on them, along with the intent that both of you work impeccably together

- New moon deity, Ixik Kab, identified as an aspect of younger Deity I*
- New moon solar eclipse deity, Cihuacoatl†

## *Wording and Intention Setting*

In *Cleansing Rites of Curanderismo,* I explain two fundamental guidelines in writing petitions. The first is to ask for an ideal outcome and trust and know that you deserve it. Most of us are not fully aware of what an ideal reality looks like and are in the process of cocreating it, so allow yourself to remain open to it. If you think there are blocks to something you believe is ideal, you definitely have the right to have them removed. Second, understand that everyone has a right to their reality, so just be concerned with your own. If something or someone is in alignment with us, they will fall into alignment with our reality.

In my petitions and invocations, I always start with "God, Company of Heaven, I Am That I Am, please and thank you, with and by the Sacred Fires of God's Light and Love, for ensuring . . ." and end with "Thank you." When I use the term *God,* it is free of any religious associations; rather, I understand it to be a divine principle of the Highest Love. The Sacred Fires of God's Love and Light clear and transmute any and all kinds of dense energies into light. If the term *God* does not resonate with you, use a term that refers to something you feel is a divine principle, one that has the power to clear and transmute, whether the prayer be to Krishna, Buddha, Hecate, or any other force or deity. Faith in a divine force or principle fuels the magic in any petition or invocation.[51]

---

*Ixik Kab has been identified with the Earth, fertility, and lunar aspects. In the Classic period, she was usually depicted with a net skirt, a rabbit, a large lunar crescent, a lunar crescent marking on her cheek, a foliation on the forehead (indicating a connection with ripe corn), and air volutes of copal going into her nose. Refer to pages 36–37 and 39 for more information on Deity I generally.

†See pages 33–34 for more information on Cihuacoatl.

## *Discovering and Manifesting New Ventures*

Connect from your sacred heart with the new moon, and thank it for helping you to discover and manifest an ideal new beginning or venture for yourself. Then engage in breathwork to cleanse and rejuvenate the mind, body, and spirit.

### Breathwork to Cleanse and Rejuvenate

Place the hands on the knees. Inhale while slowly curving the spine in, and then slowly exhale, moving the chest forward and straightening the spine, using the hands on the knees as leverage. After 30 seconds, begin inhaling and exhaling a little faster, and continue doing so every 30 seconds for up to 3 minutes, and then slow back down, also moving in 30-second increments. After 6 minutes, sit up straight with your eyes closed and ask yourself what new beginning or venture you would love to see take place in your life.

Allow yourself to simply be with the question. Imagine it gracefully swirling through each one of your chakras. While focusing on the question, see the color of the chakra and its gentle, clockwise, energetic movement. Let the question seep into your energetic bodies. Begin to feel excited about what you will discover and manifest. Trust that as you simply permit yourself to be with the question, your intuition will guide you to something extraordinary, and before you know it, opportunities will present themselves to you. Wait for the ones that feel right and even amazing.

## *Conceiving a Child*

To aid in conceiving a child, place a geranium plant in your room. Connect with the new moon and the geranium, and thank them for helping you to conceive a healthy baby. As you watch the geranium grow, nourish it with love and water, connect with the new moon, and invite life to grow within you.

## MORE ELABORATE NEW MOON RITES

### ◎ Velación *and Planting Seeds for New Beginnings*

A velación is a fire limpia rite that involves candle magic and manifesting. For this rite you will need:

- Seeds (you are welcome to use seeds you already have or any of the seeds recommended below)
- Parchment paper
- A No. 2 pencil
- A 7-day candle

Start by connecting with the new moon; if you are also working with the night sun, connect with him too. Thank them for helping to infuse your rite with their power and magic. Write your intention on a piece of parchment paper with a No. 2 pencil.

The following seeds are very magical and are excellent for fostering new beginnings. Here are some of their additional gifts:

**Flax seeds** attract financial abundance and strengthen healing intentions.

**Fennel seeds** inspire courage and cleanse the body, mind, and spirit. They also fortify the energy fields of a home.

**Sesame seeds** draw in financial abundance, success, and love and inspire awareness and realization toward our bliss.

**Caraway seeds** enhance energy fields of self and space, attract love, and inspire sensuous love.

Place the seeds in a circle on top of the parchment paper, and light a 7-day candle on top of the paper in the middle of the circle of seeds. After the candle goes out, place the paper and seeds on your altar or somewhere safe. On the next new moon night, bury the seeds and the paper.

## *Water Rite: New Beginnings and New Cycles*

Water and the moon are deeply connected, so I have included this limpia for the lunar phases, modifying the instructions for each phase. This is what you will be needing for all the limpias.

- A 4- to 8-ounce glass of water (please do not use this glass to drink from afterward)
- Incense or charcoal and resins (if you decide to burn charcoal and resin, you will also need a glazed brazier)
- Epsom salt, rubbing alcohol, and dry herbs (to cleanse the space first with a white fire limpia; see pages 81–82 for instructions)
- Parchment paper
- A No. 2 pencil
- Honey

Start the ceremony the day before the peak of the new moon. Begin by cleansing the space where the ceremony will take place with a white fire limpia. Connect with the new moon from your sacred heart; if you are also working with the night sun, connect with it too. Focus on the new beginnings or cycles you would love to realize in your life. Let yourself feel the happiness from the manifested intention. Write your intention with the pencil on the parchment paper. Hold the glass of water in your hands. Feel the happiness from the manifestation of this intention, and let this energy flow into the glass of water from your hands. Place this water on top of the petition. Light the incense. If you are using charcoal, light it and place the resins on top as an offering. Place this petition outside under the new moon or on a windowsill, where the moon's light and magic will touch the petition.

On the evening the new moon has peaked, light another stick of incense, or burn resin on a charcoal tablet. Once again, hold the glass of water in your hands. Tune in to the joy from the manifested intention, and let this energy flow into the water from your hands.

The day after the peak of the new moon, light another stick of incense, or burn resin on a charcoal tablet. Hold the glass of water in your hands one last time, and tune in to the exuberance from the manifested intention. Let this energy flow into the water from your hands.

In the morning of the next day, place the petition on your altar or somewhere safe. When you are in the shower that day, bathe yourself with the glass of water. Rub honey all over yourself, then wash off in the shower. Once the intention comes to be, bury the petition.

## WORKING WITH THE ENERGIES OF THE WAXING MOON

The ancient Mexica and Maya believed that the waxing moon emitted energies of growth, expansion, and fertility. It was typically associated with pregnant lunar deities.

Here is a list of sacred items, activities, and a lunar deity associated with the waxing moon:

- Rites to ensure growth and expansion
- Abundance rites
- Rites to ensure the healthy growth of a baby
- Expanding love or sensuous relationships
- Water rites
- Fragrant night flowers: gardenias, evening primrose, brugmansia, moonflower, nicotiana, night-blooming jasmine, and datura
- Shells
- Pyrite and emeralds: for growth and expansion
- Lunar deity, Xochiquetzal*

### *Mantras for Expansion, Increase, and Abundance*

For mantras that invite growth, expansion, and abundance, mentally focus on what you are welcoming in, and allow yourself to feel the excitement of

*See pages 32–33 for more on Xochiquetzal.

it. Interweave a statement that reflects gratitude for your continuing growth, expansion, and abundance in regard to what you are welcoming. Connect with the waxing moon by sending it love, and thank it for helping you to manifest your intention.

The next breathwork rite is a great exercise to engage in daily when reciting these types of mantras. The breathwork clears away energy and makes room for us to feel the joy, excitement, and gratitude for the manifestation of the mantra.

### Breathwork: Revitalizing and Manifestation

Place the hands in the Om mudra by joining the tip of the thumb and index finger while the other fingers are straight (see figure 7.2). Place your hands on your thighs, with the palms of your hands up. Take brisk inhales and exhales through the mouth, allowing your cheeks to expand with the exhales. Repeat this for 3 minutes, and then begin reciting your mantra.

Figure 7.2. Om mudra.
*Illustration by Carolina Gutierrez.*

## MORE ELABORATE WAXING MOON RITES

### Ofrenda de Maíz *(Offering of Corn) to Expand or Increase*

What you will need for this rite:

- 1¼ cups cornmeal
- 2½ cups water
- 2 teaspoons of honey

- Cooking pot
- Soup bowl
- At least 2 fragrant night flowers, such as gardenias, evening primrose, brugmansia, moonflower, nicotiana, night-blooming jasmine, or datura
- A small glass or vase for your flowers (put water in once you have placed the flowers in it)
- A No. 2 pencil
- Parchment paper

Begin this rite on the first day of a waxing moon. Connect from your sacred heart with the waxing moon and thank it for helping you to expand or increase whatever you are choosing. Write down your intention on a piece of parchment paper with a No. 2 pencil. Mix the cornmeal, water, honey, and one of the flowers together, and cook over a medium heat, stirring frequently, until mixture thickens, 5 to 7 minutes. Place the cornmeal in a soup bowl.

Place your petition in between the cornmeal and the other night flowers, and leave these items outside to receive moonlight, allowing the night flowers to dry. Remove your offerings and petition 2 days before the full moon. Keep the petition and dry night flowers on an altar or special place. When your intention comes true, bury them in the Earth.

## ◎ *Water Rite to Increase or Expand*

What you will need for this rite:

- A glass of water
- Incense, or resins and a charcoal tablet
- A glazed brazier (if you are using resins and charcoal)
- A No. 2 pencil
- Parchment paper
- Honey

Start the ceremony 4 days before the peak of the waxing moon. Begin by cleansing the space where the ceremony will take place with a white fire limpia. Connect with the waxing moon from your sacred heart. If you are also working with the night sun, connect with him too. Focus on what you would love to increase or expand in your life. Feel the happiness from the manifested intention. Write your intention with a No. 2 pencil on a piece of parchment paper. Hold the glass of water in your hands. Feel the happiness from the manifested intention, and let this energy flow into the glass of water from your hands. Place this water on top of the petition. Light the incense; if you are using resins, light the charcoal, and place them on top. Put this petition outside under the waxing moon or on a windowsill where the light and magic of the moon will touch the petition.

On the evening the waxing moon has peaked, light another stick of incense; if you are using resins, light another piece of charcoal and place them on top. Once again, hold the glass of water in your hands, and tune in to the joy from the manifested intention. Let this energy flow into the water from your hands. Four days after the peak of the waxing moon, light another stick of incense or a charcoal tablet and resin. Hold the glass of water in your hands one last time, and tune in to the joy from the manifested intention. Let this energy flow into the water from your hands. In the morning, place the petition on your altar or somewhere safe. When you are in the shower that day, bathe yourself with the glass of water at any stage of your shower. Then rub honey all over yourself, everywhere. Then wash off in the shower. Once the intention comes to be, bury the petition.

## WORKING WITH THE ENERGIES OF THE FULL MOON

For the ancient Mexica and Maya, the full moon facilitated successful cycles of completion and maturity. These energies were accessed one or two days before and after the full moon.

Lunar eclipses were fearful events and for the Classic Maya were times to face enemies and wage war against them. Eclipses made the unseen tzitzimime stars, enemies to the world, visible. I utilize the energies of lunar eclipses to reflect on any difficult relations and whether apologies are in order. If I am no longer in contact with this person, I light a candle and send them good wishes for peace. Facing enemies in war was a government undertaking, in which I have no interest. I am, however, interested in maintaining peaceful relations, so if someone has wronged me or vice versa, I use lunar eclipses to reflect on these relations and ask for peace and graceful resolutions.

The following is a list of sacred items, activities, and a lunar deity connected to the full moon:

- Rites to ensure successful completion
- Rites to secure an ideal maturation
- Rites to bring closure
- Selenite, white moonstone, clear calcite, clear quartz, and any golden crystals, such as golden topaz, golden aura quartz, golden Lemurian seed crystal
- Shells
- Water rites
- Lunar deity, Tlazolteotl*

## *Reflecting on Completion: Coloring*

Meditation, breathwork, and coloring are ideal rites for reflecting on completion. Art projects, such as coloring in mandalas or some other sacred geometrical image, quiet the mind and allow us to be in a trance meditative space. In this space we can more readily access intuitive information and guidance. These spaces are also ideal for reflecting on where you have been and what you have completed, as well as on what else you would love to accomplish in your life.

On the night of the next full moon, consider coloring on that night while reflecting on accomplishments and goals. Light some incense, or light a charcoal tablet and place some copal on it. Connect with the full moon and, if it feels appropriate, the night sun too. Have your mandala ready, or you

*See page 34 for more information on Tlazolteotl.

can search on the internet for a Mesoamerican glyph or artwork that you resonate with. Reflect on what you have accomplished and what else you would like to accomplish. Reflecting on tasks we have completed inspires us to complete others. During the coloring, thank the full moon for helping you to facilitate the successful completion of your goal. Thereafter, repeat mantras of gratitude for successful completion until the intention comes to pass.

## MORE ELABORATE FULL MOON RITES

### ◎ *Coming Full Circle*

For this rite you will need:

- Any 5 of the following crystals: selenite, white moonstone, clear calcite, clear quartz, and any golden crystals, such as golden topaz, golden aura quartz, or golden Lemurian seed crystal
- White piece of paper
- A No. 2 pencil
- Parchment paper
- Three incense sticks or 3 charcoal tablets and copal

Clear the crystals of any other information by placing them under running water, leaving them in a glass of water with salt overnight, or placing them inside a Tibetan bowl while playing the bowl.

On the night before the peak of the full moon, connect with the full moon, and thank it for ensuring that you come full circle or successfully complete something. Draw a circle on the white paper. Place 4 of the crystals at the circle's 4 cardinal points—east, west, north, and south.

Connect with your intention, and write it down with the pencil on the parchment paper. Place your petition in the middle of the circle, and place the fifth crystal on top of it. Place the petition outside so it can absorb and be charged by moonlight. If you are unable to do this, go outside with the crystals in your hands with palms open, lovingly ask the full moon to charge them, and leave the paper with your petition inside your home. Leave copal or incense burning next to the paper as an offering for the full moon. Offer copal or incense on the peak of the full moon, and the evening after the peak. Make sure to leave everything intact those 3 nights.

The next morning, place the petition on your altar or somewhere special, and carry the crystals with you until your intention comes to fruition. When it does, bury the petition in the Earth.

### ◎ *Water Rite to Ensure Successful Completion*

Please see page 138 for what you will need for this water limpia. Start the ceremony one evening before the peak of the full moon. Begin by cleansing the space where the water moon ceremony will take place with a white fire limpia. Connect with the full moon, and if you are also working the night sun, connect with the night sun too from your sacred heart, and focus on what you would love to ensure a successful completion for. Revel in the excitement that your intention has been realized.

Write your intention with a No. 2 pencil on a parchment paper. Hold the glass of water in your hands, and let yourself feel the happiness from the intention being manifested, and let this energy flow into the glass of water from your hands. Place this water on top of the petition. Light a stick of incense; if you are using resins, light a piece of charcoal, and place them on top. Place this petition outside under the full moon or on a windowsill where the light and magic of the moon touches the petition. Follow the instructions that are outlined above for the new moon.

## WORKING WITH THE ENERGIES OF THE WANING MOON

For the ancient Mexica and Maya, the waning moon emitted energies that helped to ensure decrease, clearing, and the death of something and was associated with aging. Interestingly, the waning moon deity was also depicted as engaging in a waning-phase rite, harvesting honey, which is associated with abundance and joy. When there is a decrease in something, there will be an increase in some other venture. I typically complement a waning rite by engaging in a rite on the next waxing moon, focusing on the increase or expansion of something, unless I am intending on cloaking and camouflaging something during the waning moon.

The following are some sacred activities, items, and a lunar deity associated with the waning moon:

- Rites to decrease
- Releasing rites
- Rites to cloak and camouflage information
- Water rites
- Shells
- Howlite, smoky quartz, black tourmaline, and black obsidian
- Grandmother lunar deity, Toci*

## *Releasing Rite*

Make a concentrated tea of rosemary, yarrow, or St. John's wort, preferably with loose-leaf or fresh herbs. Connect with the herbs and waning moon. Eat a small sprig of oregano, and while the oregano is still fresh in your mouth, state out loud or silently what you are choosing to release. Oregano inspires graceful releasing. Avoid stating comments such as "I want to release . . . " or "I would like to release . . ." Rather state releasing statements in a clear affirmative statement such as, "I release . . . and so it is."

Do this under a waning moon night or during the afternoon of a waning moon phase to get the sun's energies and power in releasing. Repeat your affirmation during this one rite. You can also couple this rite with a releasing breathwork. Interweave breathwork with stating (out loud or silently) what you are releasing; breathwork enhances the energy of releasing.

## *Releasing Breathwork*

Take a deep inhale. Gently rotate and move the shoulders side to side while rapidly exhaling. After a minute or so, move the shoulders, chest out, and

---

*See pages 32 and 68 for more on Toci.

exhale with a sharp "who" sound. Then state what you are choosing to release. Repeat this cycle for at least 5 minutes. After you feel the energy has been released, refrain from stating what you are choosing to release. Accept that it has been released, and move forward.

### *Cleansing Sacred Tools: Mugwort*

Thank the waning moon for cleansing your sacred tools, and connect with the dawn sun for revitalizing them. Make a concentrated mugwort tea. Place your sacred tools in the tea, and leave them outside during a waning moon night until morning. In the morning, run water over the tools, and as you are doing so, imbue them with your intentions. Thank the water as well for aiding you in your intention.

## MORE ELABORATE WANING MOON RITES

### *Baños to Cleanse and Release*

For this rite you will need the following items:

- Feverfew
- Coconut soap
- Three candles: yellow, green, and black, any size
- A bathtub (if you do not have a bathtub, use a child's-size pool)
- Dry herbs to cleanse the space where you will be taking the baño
- 2 cups of Epsom salt

On a waning moon night prepare a baño. (See pages 56–58 for instructions on preparing a spiritual bath.) Make a concentrated feverfew tea, and place it in the tub or pool. Place the Epsom salt in as well. Thank the waning moon, feverfew, and water for helping to cleanse and release anything or any energies that no longer serve you.

Light the 3 candles while stating what you are choosing to release. Wash your body with the coconut soap while stating what you are choosing to release. Once you feel complete, drain the water. Let the candles burn out completely on your altar or somewhere safe. Accept that you have successfully released whatever you set out to release.

## *Water Rite to Decrease and Release*

Please see page 141 for what you will need for this water limpia. Start the ceremony 4 evenings before the peak of the waning moon. Begin by cleansing the space where the water-moon ceremony will take place with a white fire limpia. Connect with the waning moon from your sacred heart. If you are also working with the night sun, connect with it too. Focus on what you want to release or decrease in your life.

Hold the glass of water in your hands, and let yourself feel the gratitude for what the moon and night sun are helping you to release and decrease in your life. Let this energy flow into the glass of water from your hands. Place this glass on top of the petition. Light a stick of incense; if you are using resins, light a piece of charcoal, and place them on top. Place this petition outside under the waning moon or on a windowsill, where the light and magic of the moon will touch the petition. Follow the instructions outlined for the waxing moon.

---

### Coming Full Circle on a Full Moon

One of my first more elaborate magical lunar rites in 2004 was rather extraordinary. I had already been working with the sun and moon to cleanse and charge my sacred limpia tools and medicine bundles. One of my mentors at the time, Don Tomas, had taught me quite a few lunar and solar rites in my then five-year mentorship period with him. But I had not yet done an elaborate magical lunar ceremony. During this phase of my curanderismo mentorship, I had already started working as an attorney, regularly volunteered at legal nonprofits, and was also still going to Quintana Roo, Mexico (Yucatán peninsula) regularly to continue my mentorship.

On the day that I got inspired to engage in this lunar ceremony,

I had volunteered to be a legal observer for the National Lawyers Guild (NLG) in support of what was becoming one of the longest supermarket strikes in U.S. history. Nearly 60,000 United Food and Commercial Workers (UFCW) union employees walked off the job for more than four months in the hopes of attaining a more just collective bargaining agreement. As a legal observer, my role was to be on the sidelines of marches and rallies ensuring that First Amendment rights were observed, while sporting my neon-green NLG cap.

Before I left for the march, I was guided to bring a couple of sage smudge sticks. Before the march started, I took off the NLG cap, lit one of my smudge sticks, and began to smudge myself. The next thing I knew I had a long line of people waiting to be smudged by me. I was very surprised, but of course, I obliged. For the most part, I had kept my curanderismo spiritual world separate and segregated from my attorney world, including my activism. But this march felt sacred, and smudging seemed appropriate. After I smudged well over fifty people, I put my NLG cap back on and took my position as a neutral observer on the sidelines.

After marching for a couple of hours, I was closer to the rally endpoint. I got on top of a sidewall, where I could sit and observe the hundreds of people marching by and initiate one of the tools for this lunar rite. I got one of the protest flyers that had the names of the CEOs of the supermarket chains on it and held it up. I sat there for almost an hour setting the intention that the energy of the protesters go into this flyer.

When I got home, I got one of my deer hide medicine bundles that had the Maya Round Calendar on it and that I had frequently brought to temazcales (sweat lodges) with me and used to charge my medicine tools and myself. I placed the following crystals at the cardinal points of my medicine bundle: a pyrite at the south, a black obsidian at the west, a white howlite at the north, and a red garnet at the east. With the help of these crystals and my medicine bundle, I set the intention that this rite take place in a sacred space. In the middle of my bundle I placed the flyer, and on top of it I placed a large pink quartz crystal and my green glass heart-shaped *sastun*. Sastun stones are identified as sacred stones by many Maya indigenous peoples and can be used in many divinatory rites, including determining the cause of someone's illness.

It was dusk with a gorgeous full moon making its presence. I lit a charcoal tablet, offered copal to my medicine bundle, and set the intention that the night sun and full moon transmute the discord between both sides and that a just collective bargaining agreement come into effect. I left my medicine bundle outside with everything intact. The next morning I offered more copal and did this again at nightfall and left my medicine bundle outside again.

The next morning I knew the moon was about to go into its waning phase. I looked around my garden to find the place where I would bury the names of the CEOs of the supermarket chains within Mother Earth. I found a random stick from my avocado tree that had a forked end that I would use as my marker so I can find where I had buried their names. I dug a small hole in the ground with this stick. I then cut out the names of the CEOs from the flyer and placed each name in the hole and buried them. I placed the stick in the ground where I had buried their names. I was guided to place my sastun at the fork end of the stick, and it happened to fit perfectly there.

Every morning and night I made copal offerings at the place where their names had been buried. The intention of burying their names in Mother Earth was to melt the hardness around their hearts so they might have more compassion for their employees with the help of our moon, sun, elements, and Mother Earth.

One morning on my way to work I heard on the Democracy Now radio show that the UFCW and CEOs were about to reenter discussions concerning the terms of the collective bargaining agreement. During lunch, I had a sinking feeling in my heart that something had happened to the space where I buried their names. I remembered my gardener was coming that day, and I had forgotten to do anything to fortify or protect my stick and sastun.

On my way home I was listening to KPFK FM news and heard that the discussion between both sides fell through. When I got home, I immediately went out to my garden and found the stick on the ground with my sastun next to it. I offered copal and put the stick back up and placed my sastun back on the forked end. I also cracked an egg on top of my sastun as an additional offering. Once again, I made offerings of copal in the mornings and evenings.

Interestingly enough, the collective bargaining agreement was signed on the next full moon; one full cycle from one full moon to the following one. Neither side considered it a victory, but it included more just terms for employees, particularly veteran employees. Although I do not feel that this lunar rite was the sole cause of the resolution, I do sense it was another catalyst. And it inspired me to continue on my path as a curandera and take the time to engage in more elaborate solar and lunar rites.

# Notes

## INTRODUCTION TO ANCIENT MESOAMERICAN SHAMANIC SOLAR AND LUNAR RITES

1. Eliade, *Patterns in Comparative Religion,* 11, 26. As defined by religious historian Mircea Eliade, a hierophany is the manifestation of the sacred in an object or event in the material world. Hierophanies can take the form of sacred sites, images, myths, and rites.
2. Ardren, *Social Identities,* 51.
3. Bell, *Ritual Theory, Ritual Practice,* 267.
4. Geertz, *Interpretation,* 112–13.
5. Bell, *Ritual,* 235, 252.
6. Foster, *Handbook,* 164.
7. Klein, "None of the Above," 201–206, 219.
8. Klein, "None of the Above," 201–206.
9. Conkey and Gero, "Programme to Practice," 416.
10. Garber, *Vested Interests,* 11.
11. Hewitt, "What's in a Name," 258; Houston et al., *The Memory of Bones,* 52.
12. Klein, "None of the Above," 190–91.
13. Looper, "Women-Men," 171.
14. Looper, "Women-Men," 172, fig. 10.1.
15. Sahagún, *Florentine Codex,* 4 & 5:3–4.
16. McCafferty and McCafferty, "Spinning and Weaving," 28; Sullivan, "Tlazolteotl-Ixcuina," 19, 22, 26.
17. Ardren, *Social Identities,* 94.
18. Aguilar-Moreno, *Handbook,* 74.

19. De Landa, *Yucatán,* 12–13; Aguilar-Moreno, *Handbook,* 74.
20. Ruiz de Alarcón, *Aztec Sorcerers,* 1, 16, 30, 32.
21. Turner, *Ritual Process,* 137–64.
22. Boone, *Cycles of Time,* 60.
23. Boone, *Cycles of Time,* 61.
24. Ardren, *Social Identities,* 16–17.
25. Ardren, *Social Identities,* 16–17.
26. Smith, *At Home with the Aztecs,* 7, 24–25, 71, 91, 96; Lohse, "Commoner Ritual," 18–19; Lucero, *Water and Ritual,* 40–41; Rothenberg, "Interpreting Plaza Spaces," 122, 128; Gonlin, "Ritual and Ideology," 89–90, 107–108.
27. Smith, *At Home with the Aztecs,* 51, 59; Gonlin, "Ritual and Ideology," 94–96.
28. Begley, *Train Your Mind,* 56, 65.
29. Davidson and Begley, *Emotional Life,* 11; Gordon and Berger, *Intelligent Memory,* 97; Orenstein, "Neural Basis," 1; Begley, *Train Your Mind,* 66, 130.
30. Kerr, et al., "Mindfulness," 1; Walton, "How to Kill a Thought," 1.
31. Univ. of N. Carolina, "Brief meditative exercise helps cognition," 1.
32. Begley, *Train Your Mind,* 66, 130.
33. Houston, Mazariegos, and Stuart, "Time," 207.
34. Teeple, "Maya Inscriptions," 243, 248.
35. Teeple, "Maya Inscriptions," 242, 254.

## 1. INTERTWINING THE ENERGIES OF THE SUN AND MOON

1. Aguilar-Moreno, *Handbook,* 304–5; Foster, *Handbook,* 247, 256.
2. Buenaflor, *Cuanderismo Soul Retrieval,* 10–11; Stuart, *Order of Days,* 82–83; Aguilar-Moreno, *Handbook,* 302–303; Foster, *Handbook,* 28.
3. Stuart, *Order of Days,* 77–82; Aguilar-Moreno, *Handbook,* 304–305.
4. Stuart, *Order of Days,* 82–83; Foster, *Handbook,* 256.
5. Mendez et al., "Astronomical Observations," 44; Milbrath, *Star Gods,* 1.
6. Carter, "Innovative Ritual," 1; Aguilar-Moreno, *Handbook,* 302; León-Portilla, *Aztec Thought,* 117–18.
7. Foster, *Handbook,* 256; Aguilar-Moreno, *Handbook,* 291.
8. Aguilar-Moreno, *Handbook,* 291.

9. Durán, *Book of Gods,* 188, 414; Sahagún, *Florentine Codex,* 2:216; 7:1.
10. Durán, *Book of Gods,* 240.
11. Sahagún, *Primeros Memoriales,* 154–55; Aguilar-Moreno, *Handbook,* 306; Sahagún, *Florentine Codex,* 7:11, 60.
12. Sahagún, *Primeros Memoriales,* 123–24, 153; Sahagún, *Florentine Codex,* 2:216.
13. Sahagún, *Florentine Codex,* 2:216; Sahagún, *Primeros Memoriales,* 80, 123–24, 153.
14. Sahagún, *Florentine Codex,* 1:241–42.
15. Maffie, *Aztec Philosophy,* 207.
16. Carrasco, *Religions,* 52.
17. Aguilar-Moreno, *Handbook,* 309.
18. Durán, *Book of Gods,* 133.
19. León-Portilla, *Aztec Thought,* 31.
20. León-Portilla, *Aztec Thought,* 50.
21. Aguilar-Moreno, *Handbook,* 138.
22. León-Portilla, *Aztec Thought,* 51–52; Aguilar-Moreno, *Handbook,* 303.
23. Sahagún, *Florentine Codex,* 7:9; Ortiz de Montellano, *Aztec Medicine,* 142–43; Aguilar-Moreno, *Handbook,* 309.
24. Sahagún, *Florentine Codex,* 7:2.
25. Taube, "The Bilimek Pulque Vessel," 12.
26. Stuart, *Order of Days,* 49–50.
27. Taube, *Legendary Past,* 33.
28. Sahagún, *Florentine Codex,* 3:1, 7:4–8; Ruiz de Alarcón, *Aztec Sorcerers,* 31, 100, 101.
29. Aguilar-Moreno, *Handbook,* 309.
30. León-Portilla, *Aztec Thought,* 98.
31. Stuart, "Face of the Calendar Stone," 7, 10; Taube, "Turquoise Hearth," 321.
32. Miller and Taube, *Illustrated Dictionary,* 60–61; Milbrath, "Decapitated Lunar Goddesses," 195–98.
33. Stuart, "Face of the Calendar Stone," 10.
34. Taube, "Turquoise Hearth," 321; Beyer, "El llamado 'calendario Azteca,'" 188–200; Sáenz, "Tres estelas de Xochicalco," 58.
35. Stuart, "Face of the Calendar Stone," 12; Umberger, *Aztec Sculptures,* 205.
36. Durán, *History of the Indies,* 191.

37. Stuart, "Face of the Calendar Stone," 1, 10.
38. Durán, *Book of Gods,* 78; Maffie, *Aztec Philosophy,* 110.
39. Aguilar-Moreno, *Handbook,* 309.
40. Aguilar-Moreno, *Handbook,* 259.
41. Sahagún, *Florentine Codex,* 2:38.
42. De Landa, *Yucatán,* 59.
43. Foster, *Handbook,* 256.
44. Mendez et al., "Astronomical Observations," 46; Aveni, *Skywatchers,* 163–214.
45. Milbrath, *Star Gods,* 74; Tedlock, *Popol Vuh* (1985), 72.
46. Milbrath, *Star Gods,* 91.
47. Milbrath, *Star Gods,* 70; Craine and Reindorp, *Codex Perez,* 49–50; Roys, *Book of Chilam Balam,* 110–111.
48. Foster, *Handbook,* 161.
49. Scherer, *Mortuary Landscapes,* 132; Taube, "Maws of Heaven and Hell," 411.
50. Taube, *Legendary Past,* 53.
51. Thompson, *Maya Hieroglyphic Writing,* 251.
52. Foster, *Handbook,* 185.
53. Taube, *Legendary Past,* 59–62; Christenson, *Popol Vuh,* 178–79; Mazariegos, "Fire and Sacrifice," 35.
54. Thompson, *Maya History,* 237; Mazariegos, "Of Birds and Insects," 51–55.
55. Foster, *Handbook,* 169.
56. Thompson, *Maya History,* 238.
57. Taube, *Major Gods,* 54–56; Taube, "Representaciones del paraíso," 36.
58. Taube, *Major Gods,* 54; Lounsbury, "Identity," 48–49.
59. Taube, *Major Gods,* 54.
60. Taube, *Major Gods,* 54–55.
61. Buenaflor, *Curanderismo Soul Retrieval,* 92; Zender, *Study,* 69; Martin, Berrin, and Miller, *Courtly Art,* 57.
62. Scherer, *Mortuary Landscapes,* 61–62, 116.
63. Vail and Bricker, "*Haab* Dates," 181.
64. Hernández and Bricker, "Inauguration," 316; Paxton, *Cosmos,* 58.
65. Foster, *Handbook,* 262.
66. Vail, "Iconography," 184–85.
67. Mendez et al., "Astronomical Observations," 51.

68. Mendez et al., "Astronomical Observations," 53, 67.
69. Mendez et al., "Astronomical Observations," 74.
70. Šprajc, "Archaeoastronomy," 27–28, 57, 70.
71. De Landa, *Yucatán,* 5, 56, 72.
72. Šprajc, "Archaeoastronomy," 27–28.
73. Dowd, "Hierophanies," 41–46.
74. Dowd, "Hierophanies," 47–48.
75. Mendez et al., "Astronomical Observations," 47.
76. Foster, *Handbook,* 235.
77. Dowd, "Hierophanies," 57; Mendez et al., "Astronomical Observations," 49.
78. Mendez et al., "Astronomical Observations," 50; Dowd, "Hierophanies," 44, table 3.1.
79. Martin, Berrin, and Miller, *Courtly Art,* 59–60; Bernatz, "God L," 166–68.
80. Carlson, "Astronomical Investigations," 107.

## 2. MESOAMERICAN SOLAR AND LUNAR DEITIES

1. Houston and Stuart, "Gods, Glyphs, and Kings," 292; Taube, *Major Gods,* 9; Aguilar-Moreno, *Handbook,* 145, 154.
2. Kellogg, *Law,* 24; Nash, "Ideology," 351–52; De Landa, *Yucatán,* 51; Ardren, *Social Identities,* 120–21, 144–46.
3. Milbrath, "Gender Roles of Lunar Deities," 52; Soustelle, *Daily Life,* 104; Thompson, *Maya History,* 245.
4. León-Portilla, *Aztec Thought,* 125; Thompson, *Maya History,* 245.
5. Maffie, *Aztec Philosophy,* 90.
6. Maffie, *Aztec Philosophy,* 272, 276, 296.
7. Aguilar-Moreno, *Handbook,* 172.
8. Sahagún, *Florentine Codex,* 3:49; León-Portilla, *Aztec Thought,* 126; Aguilar-Moreno, *Handbook,* 149, 296.
9. Durán, *Book of Gods,* 188.
10. Durán, *Book of Gods,* 187.
11. Sahagún, *Florentine Codex,* 7:5–6.
12. Boone, *Cycles of Time,* 42; Aguilar-Moreno, *Handbook,* 151.
13. Durán, *Book of Gods,* 188.
14. Aguilar-Moreno, *Handbook,* 148; Soustelle, *Daily Life,* 102.

15. Aguilar-Moreno, *Handbook,* 148; Sahagún, *Primeros Memoriales,* 94, note 4.
16. López-Austin, *Cuerpo humano,* 1:422–23.
17. Maffie, *Aztec Philosophy,* 206–207; Turner, *Cultures at the Crossroads,* 70.
18. Boone, *Cycles of Time,* 48; Maffie, *Aztec Philosophy,* 207.
19. Miller and Taube, *Illustrated Dictionary,* 190; Turner, *Cultures at the Crossroads,* 76; Milbrath, "Seasonal Imagery in Ancient Mexican Almanacs," 131.
20. Boone, *Cycles of Time,* 42.
21. Milbrath, "Seasonal Imagery," 123.
22. Milbrath, "Seasonal Imagery," 124.
23. Sahagún, *Primeros Memoriales,* 98; Sahagún, *Florentine Codex,* 1:13.
24. Sahagún, *Primeros Memoriales,* 101, 109.
25. Sahagún, *Primeros Memoriales,* 108, note 79.
26. Sullivan, "Tlazolteotl-Ixcuina," 7–8.
27. McCafferty and McCafferty, "Spinning and Weaving," 28.
28. Sahagún, *Florentine Codex,* 1:15–16; Durán, *Book of Gods,* 231.
29. Milbrath, "Gender Roles," 57; Miller and Taube, *Illustrated Dictionary,* 60–61.
30. Milbrath, "Gender Roles," 55; McCafferty and McCafferty, "Spinning and Weaving," 103; Sullivan, "Tlazolteotl-Ixcuina," 19, 22, 26.
31. Aguilar-Moreno, *Handbook,* 152; McCafferty and McCafferty, "Metamorphosis of Xochiquetzal," 103.
32. McCafferty and McCafferty, "Metamorphosis of Xochiquetzal," 103, 105, 109, 117.
33. Boone, *Cycles of Time,* 43; McCafferty and McCafferty, "Metamorphosis of Xochiquetzal," 105; Durán, *Book of Gods,* 244.
34. Sullivan, "Tlazolteotl-Ixcuina," 18.
35. Durán, *Book of Gods,* 244.
36. Milbrath, "Gender Roles," 59.
37. Miller and Taube, *Illustrated Dictionary,* 60–61; Milbrath, "Gender Roles," 64; Boone, *Cycles of Time,* 43; Aguilar-Moreno, *Handbook,* 147.
38. Klein, "None of the Above," 201.
39. Aguilar-Moreno, *Handbook,* 147; Gillespie, *Aztec Kings,* 100.
40. Miller and Taube, *Illustrated Dictionary,* 60–61; Klein, "None of the Above," 207.
41. Boone, *Cycles of Time,* 43.

42. Klein, "None of the Above," 201.
43. Klein, "None of the Above," 202.
44. Sahagún, *Florentine Codex,* 2:155–56.
45. Sahagún, *Florentine Codex,* 2:156–57.
46. Sahagún, *Florentine Codex,* 1:8–11.
47. Burkhart, *Slippery Earth,* 61–62, 92, 171–77.
48. Milbrath, "Gender Roles," 52.
49. Boone, *Cycles of Time,* 43; Aguilar-Moreno, *Handbook,* 151.
50. Aguilar-Moreno, *Handbook,* 148, 192–93; Carrasco, *Religions of Mesoamerica,* 96–97.
51. Miller and Taube, *Illustrated Dictionary,* 68; Milbrath, "Gender Roles," 63.
52. Milbrath, "Gender Roles," 63.
53. Taube, *Major Gods,* 52.
54. Taube, "Maws of Heaven and Hell," 410–13.
55. Taube, *Major Gods,* 50–54; Scherer, *Mortuary Landscapes,* 33.
56. Taube, "Maws of Heaven and Hell," 410.
57. Miller and Taube, *Illustrated Dictionary,* 106.
58. Thompson, *Maya History,* 240.
59. Taube, "At Dawn's Edge," 175–76.
60. De Landa, *Yucatán,* 33.
61. Foster, *Handbook,* 166.
62. Taube, *Major Gods,* 54.
63. Stuart and Stuart, *Palenque,* 190.
64. Stuart and Stuart, *Palenque,* 194, 209.
65. Ardren, "Mending the Past," 31–33; Taube, *Major Gods,* 60–63, 64–68, 99–105; Mazariegos, *Art and Myth,* 202–6.
66. Thompson, *Maya History,* 244; Milbrath, "Gender Roles," 77.
67. Paxton, *Cosmos,* 45; Thompson, *Maya History,* 233–35.
68. De Landa, *Yucatán,* 70; Ardren, *Social Identities,* 118–21.
69. Taube, *Major Gods,* 60–63; Milbrath, "Gender Roles," 73–74; Mazariegos, *Art and Myth,* 202–6.
70. Looper, "Women-Men," 174, 176, 178–81; Taube, *Major Gods,* 64, 67–68.
71. Hewitt, "What's in a Name," 253–56, 258; Looper, "Women-Men," 174, 176, 178–81.
72. Looper, "Women-Men," 172, fig. 10.1.

73. Milbrath, "Gender Roles," 73–74.
74. Taube, *Major Gods,* 60–63; Milbrath, "Gender Roles," 74.
75. Milbrath, "Gender Roles," 74.
76. Ardren, "Mending the Past," 31.
77. Taube, *Major Gods,* 30, figs. a–b, d–e.
78. Taube, *Major Gods,* 64.
79. Taube, *Major Gods,* 68; Ciaramella, "Lady with the Snake Headdress," 203.
80. Ciaramella, "Lady with the Snake Headdress," 203–4.
81. Coe and Stone, *Maya Glyphs,* 117.
82. Ciaramella, "Lady with the Snake Headdress," 209.
83. Milbrath, "Postclassic Maya Metaphors," 379.
84. Taube, *Major Gods,* 99, 101.
85. Ardren, "Mending the Past," 31.
86. Taube, *Major Gods,* 99.
87. Paxton, *Cosmos,* 123.
88. De Landa, *Yucatán,* 211, 218–19.
89. Milbrath, "Postclassic Maya Metaphors," 380, 388.
90. Carlson, "Maya Deluge Myth," 205; Taube, *Legendary Past,* 71–73.

## 3. DAWN, SUNRISE, AND MORNING

1. Carlsen and Prechtel, "Flowering of the Dead," 31–32; Tedlock, *Popol Vuh* (1985), 225–26; Mazariegos, "Of Birds and Insects," 49.
2. Buenaflor, *Curanderismo Soul Retrieval,* 129.
3. De Landa, *Yucatán,* 57–58; Sahagún, *Florentine Codex,* 3:49; 7:163.
4. Sahagún, *Florentine Codex,* 7:163.
5. Taube, "Flower Mountain," 80–82; Taube, "At Dawn's Edge," 147.
6. Taube, "Flower Mountain," 80, 87; Bierhorst, *Cantares,* 22.
7. Zender, "Study," 69; Martin, Berrin, and Miller, *Courtly Art,* 57.
8. Taube, *Legendary Past,* 16.
9. Sahagún, *Florentine Codex,* 2:216; *Primeros Memoriales,* 123–24, 153.
10. Sahagún, *Florentine Codex,* 1:241–42.
11. Sahagún, *Florentine Codex,* 2:194.
12. Sahagún, *Florentine Codex,* 2:219.
13. Sahagún, *Florentine Codex,* 2:16, 175; Durán, *Book of Gods,* 83.
14. Sahagún, *Florentine Codex,* 2:194.

15. Sahagún, *Florentine Codex,* 6:95; Buenaflor, *Cleansing Rites,* 67.
16. Dibble and Anderson, "Ancient Word," 75.
17. Taube, "Ancient Maya Calendrics," 18.
18. Christenson, *Popol Vuh,* 51, note 10.
19. Tedlock, *Popol Vuh* (1985), 31.
20. Roys, *Book of Chilam Balam,* 36.
21. Roys, *Ritual of the Bacabs,* 40, folios 116, 117.
22. Taube, "Symbolism of Jade," 31–32, 37; Sahagún, *Florentine Codex,* 11:221–22.
23. Sahagún, *Florentine Codex,* 11:221–22.
24. Taube, "Symbolism of Jade," 31–32, 37.
25. Taube, "Symbolism of Jade," 47.
26. Sahagún, *Florentine Codex,* 11:222.
27. Ruiz de Alarcón, *Aztec Sorcerers,* 102.
28. Sahagún, *Florentine Codex,* 7:7.
29. Taube, *Legendary Past,* 16.
30. Sahagún, *Florentine Codex,* 7:7, 56.
31. Sahagún, *Florentine Codex,* 2:39, 4–5:113.
32. Sahagún, *Florentine Codex,* 6:197–99.
33. Sahagún, *Florentine Codex,* 4–5:53, 201.
34. Sahagún, *Florentine Codex,* 4–5:2–5, 113–14.
35. Stuart, "Fire Enters His House," 375, 417–18; Ardren, *Social Identities,* 16–17; Buenaflor, *Cleansing Rites,* 153.
36. Durán, *Book of Gods,* 427.
37. Buenaflor, *Curanderismo Soul Retrieval,* 43.

## 4. HIGH NOON AND AFTERNOON

1. Tokovinine, "Western Sun," 18; Broda, *Mexican Calendar,* 33–34, 53–54; Caso, "Un problema," 106; Thompson, *Maya Hieroglyphic Writing,* 102.
2. Sahagún, *Florentine Codex,* 7:163; Aguilar-Moreno, *Handbook,* 164; Ortiz de Montellano, *Aztec Medicine,* 50, 132.
3. Soustelle, *Daily Life,* 102.
4. Sahagún, *Florentine Codex,* 2:38.
5. Taube, "Turquoise Hearth," 321.
6. Tokovinine, "Western Sun," 18; Broda, *Mexican Calendar,* 33–34, 53–54; Caso, "Un problema," 106.

7. Thompson, *Maya Hieroglyphic Writing,* 102.
8. Durán, *Book of Gods,* 188, 191, 419; Sahagún, *Florentine Codex,* 7:31, 1:31–32, 2:177, 193, 3:66; Soustelle, *Daily Life,* 149.
9. Soustelle, *Daily Life,* 149.
10. Sahagún, *Florentine Codex,* 2:96–97.
11. Turner, *Cultures,* 70, note 10.
12. Durán, *Book of Gods,* 188, 414; Sahagún, *Florentine Codex,* 7: 1.
13. Sahagún, *Florentine Codex,* 7:163; Aguilar-Moreno, *Handbook,* 164; Ortiz de Montellano, *Aztec Medicine,* 50, 132.
14. Ortiz de Montellano, *Aztec Medicine,* 54.
15. Sahagún, *Florentine Codex,* 6:167.
16. Aguilar-Moreno, *Handbook,* 164.
17. Furst, *Natural History,* 113.
18. Sahagún, *Florentine Codex,* 7:118; Soustelle, *Daily Life,* 156.
19. Aguilar-Moreno, *Handbook,* 356.
20. Taube, "Birth Vase," 657–58.
21. Paxton, *Cosmos,* 55; Houston et al., *Memory of Bones,*, 49.
22. Mazariegos, "Of Birds and Insects," 49–51; Mazariegos, "Fire and Sacrifice," 40–43.
23. Sahagún, *Florentine Codex,* 2:115–16.
24. Durán, *Book of Gods,* 449; Burkhart, *Slippery Earth,* 120–21.
25. Sahagún, *Florentine Codex,* 2:118.
26. Boone, *Cycles of Time,* 43.

## 5. SUNSET, DUSK, AND NIGHTFALL

1. Aguilar-Moreno, *Handbook,* 304, 306.
2. Buenaflor, *Curanderismo Soul Retrieval,* 90–91; Stuart, *Order of Days,* 90; Foster, *Handbook,* 161; Brady and Ashmore, "Mountains, Caves, Water," 127.
3. Buenaflor, *Curanderismo Soul Retrieval,* 90–91.
4. De Landa, *Yucatán,* 59; Aguilar-Moreno, *Handbook,* 306–8; Milbrath, *Star Gods,* 249, 258, 261–68, 270–74.
5. Boone, *Cycles of Time,* 189.
6. Thompson, *Maya Hieroglyphic Writing,* 173.
7. Boone, *Cycles of Time,* 197; Anders, Jansen, and Reyes García, *Los templos,* 222. Boone notes that Anders, Jansen, and Reyes García interpret the olla

in the image as a drum. She concurs, because its lips are outlined with jaguar pelt markings, which suggests that it is covered with jaguar skin. The speech scrolls and little jeweled bar coming from Stripe Eye's mouth indicate that he is singing: Boone, 268, note 46.

8. Boone, *Cycles of Time,* 197.
9. Boone, *Cycles of Time,* 199.
10. Sahagún, *Primeros Memoriales,* 61, note 28.
11. Durán, *Book of Gods,* 204, 445.
12. Sahagún, *Primeros Memoriales,* 61–62.
13. Durán, *Book of Gods,* 83.
14. Durán, *Book of Gods,* 107.
15. Durán, *Book of Gods,* 423.
16. Scherer, *Mortuary Landscapes,* 132; Taube, "Maws of Heaven and Hell," 411.
17. Taube, "Maws of Heaven and Hell," 406.
18. Taube, "Maws of Heaven and Hell," 413.
19. Tokovinine, "The Western Sun," 17; Mathews, "The Inscription," 404–7.
20. Tokovinine, "The Western Sun," 18.
21. Watanabe, "In the World of the Sun," 723; Tokovinine, "The Western Sun," 19.
22. Tokovinine, "The Western Sun," 20.
23. Durán, *Book of Gods,* 241, 450.
24. Sahagún, *Florentine Codex,* 2:21–22.
25. Sahagún, *Florentine Codex,* 2: 15, 17, 27, 57, 101, 109–10, 165, 175.
26. Durán, *Book of Gods,* 214–15.
27. Sahagún, *Primeros Memoriales,* 59.
28. Sahagún, *Florentine Codex,* 2:14.
29. Sahagún, *Florentine Codex,* 2:141.
30. Sahagún, *Florentine Codex,* 2:136.
31. Sahagún, *Florentine Codex,* 6:129.
32. Sahagún, *Florentine Codex,* 2:40–41, 4 and 5:131–32.
33. Boone, *Cycles of Time,* 55.
34. Boone, *Cycles of Time,* 62; Taube, "The Bilimek Pulque Vessel," 3.
35. Sahagún, *Florentine Codex,* 2:21, 95, 110, 168; 4 and 5:47.
36. De Landa, *Yucatán,* 59.
37. Taube, *Legendary Past,* 53.

38. Thompson, *Maya Hieroglyphic Writing,* 11.
39. Scherer, *Mortuary Landscapes,* 132; Taube, "Maws of Heaven and Hell," 411.
40. Thompson, *Maya Hieroglyphic Writing,* 42.
41. De Landa, *Yucatán,* 67.
42. De Landa, *Yucatán,* 73–74.

## 6. MIDNIGHT AND PREDAWN

1. Taube, *Legendary Past,* 16.
2. Boone, *Cycles of Time,* 44–45; Taube, *Major Gods,* 54–55; Thompson, *Maya Hieroglyphic Writing,* 11, 74.
3. Buenaflor, *Curanderismo Soul Retrieval,* 112–15.
4. Aguilar-Moreno, *Handbook,* 291.
5. Ortiz de Montellano, *Aztec Medicine,* 153; Maffie, *Aztec Philosophy,* 60–61.
6. Sahagún, *Primeros Memoriales,*, 10, 176–77; *Florentine Codex,* 6:194.
7. Sahagún, *Florentine Codex,* 4–5:143–44.
8. Sahagún, *Florentine Codex,* 2:33, 159, 165–66.
9. Sahagún, *Florentine Codex,* 2:159–60.
10. Sahagún, *Florentine Codex,* 2:205; *Primeros Memoriales,* 80.
11. Sahagún, *Florentine Codex,* 3:66.
12. Sahagún, *Florentine Codex,* 2:141–42.
13. Durán, *Book of Gods,* 81–83, 84.
14. Durán, *Book of Gods,* 241; Sahagún, *Primeros Memoriales,* 63.
15. Sahagún, *Florentine Codex,* 2:22.
16. Milbrath, "Seasonal Imagery," 118–20; Sahagún, *Florentine Codex,* 7:12.
17. Milbrath, "Seasonal Imagery," 118–20.
18. Milbrath, "Seasonal Imagery," 118.
19. Milbrath, "Seasonal Imagery," 119; Thompson, *Maya Hieroglyphic Writing,* 75.
20. Milbrath, "Seasonal Imagery," 132.
21. Sahagún, *Florentine Codex,* 7:12.
22. Milbrath, "Seasonal Imagery," 135.
23. Mathiowetz, et al., "The Darts of Dawn," 6.
24. Sahagún, *Florentine Codex,* 7:12.
25. Durán, *Book of Gods,* 245.

26. Sahagún, *Florentine Codex,* 6:95, 109, 121.
27. Sahagún, *Florentine Codex,* 2:194; *Primeros Memoriales,* 70.
28. Sahagún, *Florentine Codex,* 2:199.
29. Sahagún, *Florentine Codex,* 7:11, 60.
30. LaBerge and Rheingold, *Exploring,* 20–22; Love, *Are You Dreaming?,* 42; Tucillo, Zeizel, and Peisel, *Field Guide,* 48.
31. LaBerge and Rheingold, *Exploring,* 22, 36; Love, *Are You Dreaming?,* 44–45.
32. Sahagún, *Primeros Memoriales,* 10.
33. Sahagún, *Primeros Memoriales,* 176–77.

## 7. RITES FOR LUNAR PHASES

1. Durán, *Book of Gods,* 133, Šprajc, "Archaeoastronomy," 27–28.
2. Milbrath, *Star Gods,* 105; Clancy, "Ancient Maya Moon," 231; Grube, "Forms of Glyph X," 1.
3. Clancy, "Ancient Maya Moon," 231.
4. Milbrath, *Star Gods,* 105; Sahagún, *Florentine Codex,* 7:3; Mendez et al., "Astronomical Observations," 74–75.
5. Milbrath, *Star Gods,* 105, 155, 185, 195, 202.
6. Sahagún, *Florentine Codex,* 7:3; Paxton, *Cosmos,* 55.
7. Mendez et al., "Astronomical Observations," 74–75; Sahagún, *Florentine Codex,* 7:3.
8. Milbrath, *Star Gods,* 140, 123, fig. e.
9. Milbrath, *Star Gods,* 138; Sahagún, *Florentine Codex,* 7:3; Paxton, *Cosmos,* 55; Báez-Jorge, *Los oficios,* 247; Milbrath, "Decapitated Lunar Goddesses," 187.
10. Sahagún, *Florentine Codex,* 7:6–7.
11. Sahagún, *Florentine Codex,* 7:3.
12. Milbrath, *Star Gods,* 105; Mendez et al., "Astronomical Observations," 51, 74–75.
13. Milbrath, "Gender Roles," 78; Báez-Jorge, *Los oficios,* 247.
14. Ardren, *Social Identities,* 102.
15. Taube, *Major Gods,* 67, fig. e, 68.
16. Thompson, *Maya Hieroglyphic Writing,* 70–73.
17. Taube, "Through a Glass," 293–94, 306.

18. Coe and Stone, *Maya Glyphs,* 63; Grube, "Forms of Glyph X," 12.
19. Mendez et al., "Astronomical Observations," 51, 74–75; Milbrath, *Star Gods,* 110.
20. Milbrath, "Decapitated Lunar Goddesses," 185.
21. Milbrath, "Decapitated Lunar Goddesses," 198; Tezozómoc, *Cronica Mexicana,* 486.
22. Milbrath, "Decapitated Lunar Goddesses," 197; Klein, "Rethinking Cihuacoatl," 243, 248–49.
23. Klein, "Devil and the Skirt," 23–27.
24. Milbrath, *Star Gods,* 143.
25. Thompson, *Maya Hieroglyphic Writing,* 77–78.
26. Sahagún, *Florentine Codex,* 7:3.
27. Milbrath, "Seasonal Calendar," 150.
28. Boone, *Cycles of Time,* 204.
29. Paxton, *Cosmos,* 55; Milbrath, *Star Gods,* 138.
30. Milbrath, *Star Gods,* 140–41.
31. Sahagún, *Florentine Codex,* 7:3.
32. Milbrath, *Star Gods,* 73; Tedlock, *Popol Vuh* (1985), 296–97, 328, 368–69.
33. Milbrath, "Postclassic Maya Metaphors," 388.
34. Ciaramella, "Lady with the Snake Headdress," 203–4.
35. Thompson, *Maya Hieroglyphic Writing,* 81, 89.
36. Mendez et al., "Astronomical Observations," 53, 72.
37. Mendez et al., "Astronomical Observations," 72.
38. Buenaflor, *Cleansing Rites of Curanderismo,* 89–90; Stuart, "Fire Enters His House," 395; Stuart and Stuart, *Palenque,* 226–28.
39. Mendez et al., "Astronomical Observations," 72.
40. Mendez et al., "Astronomical Observations," 75; Zender, "Study," 69; Martin, Berrin, and Miller, *Courtly Art,* 57.
41. Milbrath, "Decapitated Lunar Goddesses," 193–95; Aguilar-Moreno, *Handbook,* 192–93.
42. Mendez et al., "Astronomical Observations," 72–73; Schele and Freidel, *Forest of Kings,* 251.
43. Sahagún, *Florentine Codex,* 7:3, 39–40.
44. Milbrath, *Star Gods,* 187; Báez-Jorge, *Los oficios,* 247.
45. Paxton, *Cosmos,* 55; Milbrath, *Star Gods,* 141.
46. Milbrath, *Star Gods,* 141; Tedlock, *Popol Vuh* (1985), 40, 369.

47. Looper, "Women-Men," 171.
48. Taube, *Major Gods,* 64.
49. Milbrath, *Star Gods,* 141; Báez-Jorge, *Los oficios,* 247–48.
50. Scherer, *Mortuary Landscapes,* 116–17, 169.
51. Buenaflor, *Cleansing Rites of Curanderismo,* 101–2.

# Bibliography

Aguilar-Moreno, Manuel. *Handbook to Life in the Aztec World.* 1st ed. Oxford: Oxford University Press, 2006.

Anders, Ferdinand, Maarten Jansen, and Luis Reyes García. *Los templos del cielo y de la oscuridad, oráculos y liturgia: Libro explicativo del llamado Códice Borbónico.* Accompanied by a facsimile of the codex. Graz: Akademische Druck-u Verlagsanstalt; Madrid: Sociedad Estatal Quinto Centenario; Mexico City: Fondo de Cultura Económica, 1993.

Ardren, Traci. "Mending the Past: Ix Chel and the Invention of a Modern Pop Goddess." *Antiquity* 80 (2006): 25–37.

———. *Social Identities in the Classic Maya Northern Lowlands: Gender, Age, Memory, and Place.* Austin: University of Texas Press, 2015.

Aveni, Anthony F. *Skywatchers: A Revised and Updated Version of Skywatchers of Ancient Mexico.* Austin: University of Texas Press, 2001.

Báez-Jorge, Felix. *Los oficios de las diosas.* Xalapa, Mexico: Universidad Veracruzana, 1988.

Begley, Sharon. *Train Your Mind, Change Your Brain: How a New Science Reveals Our Extraordinary Potential to Transform Ourselves.* New York: Random House, 2008.

Bell, Catherine. *Ritual: Perspectives and Dimensions.* New York: Oxford University Press, 1997.

———. *Ritual Theory, Ritual Practice.* New York: Oxford University Press, 1992.

Bernatz, Michele M. "Redefining God L: The Spatial Realm of a Maya Earth Lord." In *Maya Imagery, Architecture, and Activity: Space and Spatial Analysis in Art History,* edited by Maline D. Werne-Rude and Kayle R. Spencer, 140–77. Albuquerque: University of New Mexico Press, 2015.

Beyer, Hermann. "El llamado 'calendario Axteca': Descripción e interpretación del cuauhxicalli de la 'Casa de las Águilas.'" *El México Antiguo* 10 (1965): 134–256.

Bierhorst, John. *Cantares Mexicanos: Songs of the Aztecs*. Stanford, Calif.: Stanford University Press, 1985.

Boone, Elizabeth H. *Cycles of Time and Meaning in the Mexican Books of Fate*. Austin: University of Texas Press, 2007.

Brady, James E., and Wendy Ashmore. "Mountains, Caves, Water: Ideational Landscapes of the Ancient Maya." In *Archaeologies of Landscape: Contemporary Perspectives,* edited by Wendy Ashmore and A. Bernard Knapp, 124–45. Malden, Mass.: Blackwell, 1999.

Broda, Johanna. *The Mexican Calendar as Compared to Other Mesoamerican Systems (Acta ethnologica et linguistica, Nr. 15. Series americana, 4)*. Vienna: Engelbert Stiglmayr, 1969.

Buenaflor, Erika. *Cleansing Rites of Curanderismo: Limpias Espirituales of Ancient Mesoamerican Shamans*. Rochester, Vt.: Bear & Company, 2018.

———. *Curanderismo Soul Retrieval: Ancient Shamanic Wisdom to Restore the Sacred Energy of the Soul*. Rochester, Vt.: Bear & Company, 2019.

Burkhart, Louise M. *The Slippery Earth: Nahua-Christian Moral Dialogue in Sixteenth-Century Mexico*. Tucson: University of Arizona Press, 1989.

Carlsen, Robert S., and Martin Prechtel. "The Flowering of the Dead: An Interpretation of Highland Maya Culture." *Man* 26 (1991): 23–42.

Carlson, John B. "Astronomical Investigations and Site Orientation Influences at Palenque." In *The Art, Iconography, and Dynastic History of Palenque, Part II,* edited by Merle Greene Robertson, 107–17. Pebble Beach, Calif.: The Robert Stevenson School, 1976.

———. "The Maya Deluge Myth and Dresden Codex Page 74: Not the End but the Eternal Regeneration of the World." In Dowd and Milbrath: 197–228.

Carrasco, Davíd. *Religions of Mesoamerica*. 2d ed. Long Grove, Ill.: Waveland Press, 2014.

Carter, Nicholas P. "An Innovative Ritual Cycle at Terminal Classic Ceibal." Maya Decipherment: Ideas on Ancient Maya Writing and Iconography (website), Sept. 17, 2015.

Caso, Alfonso. "Un problema de interpretación." *Yan: Ciencias Antropológicas* 2 (1954): 105–7.

Christenson, Allen J., ed. and trans. *Popol Vuh: Sacred Book of the Quiché Maya People*. Mesoweb (website), 2003.

Ciaramella, Mary. "The Lady with the Snake Headdress." In *Seventh Palenque Round Table,* edited by Merle Green Robertson and Virginia M. Fields, 201–9. San Francisco: Pre-Columbian Art Research Institute, 1994.

Clancy, Flora S. "The Ancient Maya Moon: Calendar and Character," In Dowd and Milbrath: 229–48.

Coe, Michael D., and Mark Van Stone. *Reading the Maya Glyphs.* 2d ed. London: Thames & Hudson, 2005.

Conkey, Margaret W., and Joan M. Gero. "Programme to Practice: Gender and Feminism in Archaeology," *Annual Review of Anthropology* 26 (1997): 411–37.

Craine, Eugene R., and Reginald C. Reindorp. *The Codex Perez and the Book of Chilam Balam of Maní.* Norman: University of Oklahoma Press, 1979.

Davidson, Richard J. and Begley, Sharon. *The Emotional Life of Your Brain: How Its Unique Patterns Affect the Way You Think, Feel, and Live—and How You Can Change Them.* New York: Avery Publishing, 2012.

De Landa, Diego. *Yucatán before and after the Conquest.* Translated by William Gates. New York: Dover, 1978.

Dibble, Charles E., and Arthur J. O. Anderson. "The Ancient Word." In León-Portilla, *Native Mesoamerican Spirituality*: 61–98.

Dowd, Anne S. "Maya Architectural Hierophanies." In Dowd and Milbrath: 37–76.

Dowd, Anne S., and Susan Milbrath, eds. *Cosmology, Calendars, and Horizon-Based Astronomy in Ancient Mesoamerica.* Boulder: University Press of Colorado, 2015.

Durán, Diego. *The Book of Gods and Rites and the Ancient Calendar.* Translated by F. Horcasitas and Doris Heyden. Norman: University of Oklahoma Press, 1971.

———. *The History of the Indies of New Spain.* Translated by Doris Heyden. Norman: University of Oklahoma Press, 1994.

Eliade, Mircea. *Patterns in Comparative Religion.* Cleveland: Meridian Books, 1963.

Foster, Lynn V. *Handbook to Life in the Ancient Maya World.* Oxford: Oxford University Press, 2002.

Furst, Jill Leslie McKeever. *The Natural History of the Soul in Ancient Mexico.* New Haven, Conn.: Yale University Press, 1995.

Garber, Marjorie. *Vested Interests, Cross-Dressing, and Cultural Anxiety.* New York: Routledge, 1992.

Geertz, Clifford. *Interpretation of Cultures.* New York: Basic Books, 1973.

Gillespie, Susan. *The Aztec Kings: The Construction of Rulership in Mexica History.* Tucson: University of Arizona Press, 1992.

Gonlin, Nancy. "Ritual and Ideology among Classic Maya Rural Commoners at Copán, Honduras." In Gonlin and Lohse, 83–122.

Gonlin, Nancy, and Jon C. Lohse, eds. *Commoner Ritual and Ideology in Ancient Mesoamerica.* Boulder: University Press of Colorado, 2007.

Gordon, Barry, and Lisa Berger. *Intelligent Memory: Improve the Memory That Makes You Smarter.* New York: Viking, 2003.

Grube, Nikolai, "The Forms of Glyph X of the Lunar Series." *Textdatenbank und Wörterbuch des Klassischen Maya*, research note 9 (March 12, 2018): 1–15.

Hernández, Christine, and Victoria R. Bricker. "The Inauguration of Planting in the Borgia and Madrid Codices." In Vail and Aveni: 277–320.

Hewitt, Erika. "What's in a Name: Gender, Power and Classic Maya Women Rulers." *Ancient Mesoamerica* 10, no. 2 (1999), 251–62.

Houston, Stephen, and David Stuart. "Of Gods, Glyphs, and Kings: Divinity and Rulership among the Classic Maya." *Antiquity* 70, no. 268 (1996), 289–312.

Houston, Stephen D., Oswaldo Chinchilla Mazariegos, and David Stuart, "Time." In *The Decipherment of Ancient Maya Writing*, edited by Stephen D. Houston, Oswaldo Chinchilla Mazariegos, and David Stuart, 207–9. Norman: University of Oklahoma Press, 2001.

Houston, Stephen D., David Stuart, and Karl A. Taube. *The Memory of Bones: Body, Being, and Experience among the Classic Maya.* Austin: University of Texas Press, 2011.

Kellogg, Susan. *Law and the Transformation of Aztec Culture, 1500–1700.* Norman: University of Oklahoma Press, 1995.

Kerr, Catherine E., Matthew D. Sacchet, Sara W. Lazar, Christopher I. Moore, and Stephanie R. Jones. "Mindfulness Starts with the Body: Somatosensory Attention and Top-down Modulation of Cortical Alpha Rhythms in Mindfulness Meditation." Frontiers in Human Neuroscience (website), Feb. 13, 2013.

Klein, Cecilia F. "The Devil and the Skirt: An Iconographic Inquiry into the Prehispanic Nature of the Tzitzimime." *Estudios de Cultura Náhuatl.*+ 31 (2000): 17–62.

———. "None of the Above." In *Gender in Pre-Hispanic America: A Symposium at Dumbarton Oaks, 12–13 October 1996,* edited by Cecilia F. Klein, 183–253. Washington, D.C.: Dumbarton Oaks, 2001.

———. "Rethinking Cihuacoatl: Aztec Political Imagery of the Conquered Woman." In *Smoke and Mist: Mesoamerican Studies on Memory of Thelma D. Sullivan,* edited by J. Kathryn Josserand and Karin Dankin, 237–78. Oxford: British Archeological Reports, 1988.

LaBerge, Stephen, and Howard Rheingold. *Exploring the World of Lucid Dreaming.* New York: Ballantine, 1990.

León-Portilla, Miguel. *Aztec Thought and Culture: A Study of the Ancient Nahuatl Mind.* Translated by Jack Emory Davis. Norman: University of Oklahoma Press, 1963.

———, ed. *Native Mesoamerican Spirituality: Ancient Myths, Discourses, Stories, Doctrines, Myths, Poems from the Aztec, Yucatec, Quiche-Maya and Other Sacred Traditions.* New York: Paulist, 1980.

León-Portilla, Miguel, Earl Shorris, Sylvia S. Shorris, Ascensión H. de León-Portilla, and Jorge Klor de Alva. *In the Language of Kings: An Anthology of Mesoamerican Literature, Pre-Columbian to the Present.* London: Norton, 2001.

Lohse, Jon C. "Commoner Ritual, Commoner Ideology: (Sub-)Alternate Views of Social Complexity in Prehispanic Mesoamerica." In Gonlin and Lohse: 1–32.

Looper, G. Matthew. "Women-Men (and Men-Women): Classic Maya Rules and the Third Gender." In *Ancient Maya Women,* edited by Traci Ardren, 171–202. Walnut Creek, Calif.: AltaMira Press, 2002.

López-Austin, Alfredo. *Cuerpo humano e ideología: Las concepciones de los antiguos nahuas.* 2 vols. Mexico City: Instituto de Investigaciones Antropológicas, 1984.

Lounsbury, Floyd. "The Identity of the Mythological Figures in the Cross Group Inscriptions of Palenque." In *Fourth Palenque Round Table, 1980.* Vol VI, edited by Merle Greene Robertson and Elizabeth P. Benson, 45–58. San Francisco: Pre-Columbian Art Research Institute, 1985.

Love, Daniel. *Are You Dreaming?: Exploring Lucid Dreams: A Comprehensive Guide.* Exeter, UK: Enchanted Loom Publishing, 2013.

Lucero, Lisa. *Water and Ritual: The Rise and Fall of Classic Maya Rulers.* Austin: University of Texas Press, 2006.

Maffie, James. *Aztec Philosophy: Understanding a World in Motion.* Boulder: University Press of Colorado, 2014.

Martin, Simon, Kathleen Berrin, and Mary Miller. *Courtly Art of the Ancient Maya*. New York: Thames & Hudson, 2004.

Mathews, Peter. "The Inscription on the Back of Stela 8, Dos Pilas, Guatemala." In *The Decipherment of Maya Hieroglyphic Writing,* edited by Stephen D. Houston, David Stuart, and Oswaldo Chinchilla Mazariegos, 94–115. Norman: University of Oklahoma Press, 2001.

Mathiowetz, Michael, Polly Schaafsma, Jeremy Coltman, and Karl Taube. "The Darts of Dawn: The Tlahuizcalpantecuhtli Venus Complex in the Iconography of Mesoamerica and the American Southwest." *Journal of the Southwest* 57, no. 1 (Spring 2015): 1–102.

Mazariegos, Oswaldo C. *Art and Myth of the Ancient Maya*. New Haven, Conn.: Yale University Press, 2017.

———. "Of Birds and Insects: The Hummingbird Myth in Ancient Mesoamerica." *Ancient Mesoamerica* 21 (2010): 45–61.

———. "Fire and Sacrifice in Mesoamerican Myths and Rituals." In *Smoke, Flames, and the Human Body in Mesoamerican Ritual Practice,* edited by Andrew Scherer and Vera Tiesler, 29–53. Washington, D.C.: Dumbarton Oaks, 2018.

McCafferty, Sharisse D., and Geoffrey McCafferty. "The Metamorphosis of Xochiquetzal: A Window on Womanhood in Pre- and Post-Conquest Mexico." In *Manifesting Power: Gender and Interpretation of Power in Archaeology,* edited by Tracy L. Sweely, 103–25. New York: Routledge, 1999.

———. "Spinning and Weaving as Female Gender Identity in Postclassic Mexico." In *Textile Traditions of Mesoamerica and the Andes,* edited by Margot Blum Schevill, Janet Catherine Berlo, and Edward B. Dwyer, 19–44. New York: Garland, 1991.

Mendez, Alonso, Edwin L. Barnhart, Christopher Powell, and Carol Karasik. "Astronomical Observations from the Temple of the Sun." *Archaeoastronomy* 19 (2005): 44–73.

Milbrath, Susan. "Decapitated Lunar Goddesses in Aztec Art, Myth, and Ritual." *Ancient Mesoamerica* 8 (1997), 185–206.

———. "Gender Roles of Lunar Deities in Postclassic Central Mexico and Their Correlations with the Maya Area." *Estudios de Cultura Nahuatl* 25 (1995): 45–93.

———. "Postclassic Maya Metaphors for Lunar Motion." In *Eighth Palenque*

*Round Table, 1993,* edited by Martha J. Macri and Jan McHargue, 379–92. San Francisco: Pre-Columbian Art Research Institute, 1996.

———. "A Seasonal Calendar in the Codex Borgia." In Dowd and Milbrath: 139–62.

———. "Seasonal Imagery in Ancient Mexican Almanacs of the Dresden Codex and Codex Borgia." In *Das Bild der Jahreszeiten im Wandel der Kulturen und Zeiten*, edited by Thierry Greub, 117–42. Munich: Wilhelm Fink Verlag, 2013.

———. *Star Gods of the Maya: Astronomy in Art, Folklore, and Calendars.* 1st ed. Austin: University of Texas Press, 1999.

Miller, Mary E., and Taube, Karl A. *An Illustrated Dictionary of the Gods and Symbols of Ancient Mexico and the Maya*. London: Thames & Hudson, 1997.

Muñoz Camargo, Diego. *Historia de Tlaxcala*. México: Oficina tip. de la Secretaría de foment, 1892.

Nash, June. "The Aztecs and the Ideology of Male Dominance." *Signs* 4 (1978), 349–62.

Orenstein, David. "A Neural Basis for Benefits of Meditation." News from Brown University (website), Feb. 13, 2013.

Ortiz de Montellano, Bernard R. *Aztec Medicine, Health, and Nutrition*. New Brunswick, N.J.: Rutgers University Press, 1990.

Paxton, Meredith. *The Cosmos of the Yucatec Maya: Cycles and Steps from the Madrid Codex*. Albuquerque: University of New Mexico Press, 2001.

Rothenberg, Kara A. "Interpreting Plaza Spaces Using Soil Chemistry: The View from Honduras." In *Mesoamerican Plazas: Arenas of Community and Power,* edited by Kenichiro Tsukamoto and Takeshi Inomata, 121–29. Tucson: University of Arizona Press, 2014.

Roys, Ralph L., ed. and trans. *The Book of Chilam Balam of Chumayel*. 2d ed. Norman: University of Oklahoma Press, 1967.

———. *Ritual of the Bacabs*. Norman: University of Oklahoma Press, 1965.

Ruiz de Alarcón, Hernando. *Aztec Sorcerers in Seventeenth-Century Mexico: The Treatise on Superstitions by Hernando Ruiz de Alarcón*, Translated by M. D. Coe and C. Whittaker. Albany: State University of New York Press, 1982.

Sáenz, César A. "Tres estelas de Xochicalco." *Revista Mexicana de Estudios Antropológicos* 17 (1961): 39–65.

Sahagún, Bernardino de. *Florentine Codex: General History of the Things of New*

*Spain*. 2d ed. Translated by Arthur J. O. Anderson and Charles E. Dibble. 12 vols. Santa Fe, N.M.: School of American Research and University of Utah, 2012.

———. *The Primeros Memoriales of Fray Bernardino de Sahagún*. Translated by Thelma D. Sullivan. Edited by H. B. Nicolson, Arthur J. O. Anderson, Charles E. Dibble, Eloise Quiñones Keber, and Wayne Ruwet. Norman: University of Oklahoma Press, 1997.

Schele, Linda, and David Freidel. *A Forest of Kings: The Untold Story of the Ancient Maya*. New York: William Morrow, 1990.

Scherer, Andrew K. *Mortuary Landscapes of the Classic Maya: Rituals of Body and Soul*. Austin: University of Texas Press, 2015.

Smith, Michael E. *At Home with the Aztecs: An Archaeologist Uncovers Their Daily Life*. London: Routledge Taylor and Francis, 2016.

Soustelle, Jacques. *Daily Life of the Aztecs on the Eve of the Spanish Conquest*. Translated by Patrick O'Brien. Stanford, Calif.: Stanford University Press, 1961.

Šprajc, Ivan. "The Role of Archaeoastronomy in the Maya World: The Case Study of the Island of Cozumel." *UNESCO* (2016): 57–84.

Stuart, David. "The Face of the Calendar Stone: A New Interpretation." Maya Decipherment: Ideas on Ancient Maya Writing and Iconography (website), June 13, 2016.

———. "The Fire Enters His House: Architecture and Ritual in Classic Maya Texts." In *Function and Meaning in Classic Maya Architecture*, edited by Stephen D. Houston, 373–425. Washington, D.C.: Dumbarton Oaks, 1998.

———. *The Order of Days: Unlocking the Secrets of the Ancient Maya*. New York: Three Rivers, 2011.

Stuart, David, and George Stuart. *Palenque: Eternal City of the Maya*. New York: Thames & Hudson, 2008.

Sullivan, Thelma D. "Tlazolteotl-Ixcuina: The Great Spinner and Weaver." In *The Art and Iconography of Late Postclassic Central Mexico: A Conference at Dumbarton Oaks, October 22–23, 1977*, edited by Elizabeth Hill Boone and Elizabeth P. Benson, 7–35. Washington, D.C.: Dumbarton Oaks, 1982.

Taube, Karl A. "Ancient Maya Calendrics, Cosmology, and Creation: 2012 and Beyond." *Backdirt: Annual Review of the Cotsen Institute of Archaeology at UCLA* (2012): 10–21.

———. "The Bilimek Pulque Vessel: Starlore, Calendrics, and Cosmology of Late Postclassic Central Mexico." *Ancient Mesoamerica* 4 (1993): 1–15.

———. "The Birth Vase: Natal Imagery in Ancient Maya Myth and Ritual." In *The Maya Vase Book,* Vol. 4, edited by Justin Kerr, 650–85. New York: Kerr Associates, 1994.

———. "At Dawn's Edge: Tulúm, Santa Rita, and Floral Symbolism in the International Style of Late Postclassic Mesoamerica." In *Astronomers, Scribes, and Priests: Intellectual Interchange between the Northern Maya Lowlands and Highland Mexico in the Late Postclassic Period,* edited by Gabrielle Vail and Christine Hernández, 145–91. Washington, DC: Dumbarton Oaks, 2010.

———. "Flower Mountain: Concepts of Life, Beauty, and Paradise among the Classic Maya." *RES: Anthropology and Aesthetics* 45 (Spring 2004): 69–98.

———. *The Legendary Past: Aztec and Maya Myths.* Austin: University of Texas Press, 1993.

———. *The Major Gods of Ancient Yucatán: Studies in Pre-Columbian Art and Archaeology, no. 32.* Washington, D.C.: Dumbarton Oaks, 1992.

———. "Maws of Heaven and Hell: The Symbolism of the Centipede and Serpent in Classic Maya Religion." In *Antropologia de la eternidad: La Muerte en la cultura maya,* edited by Andrés Ciudad Ruiz, Maria Humberto Ruz Sosa, and María Josefa Iglesias Ponce de León, 404–42. Madrid: Sociedad de Española de Estudios Vayas, 2003.

———. "Representaciones del paraíso en el arte cerámico del Clásico Temprano de Escuintla, Guatemala." *Iconografía y escritura teotihuacana en la costa sur de Guatemala y Chiapas* 1, no. 5. (2005): 33–54.

———. "The Symbolism of Jade in Classic Maya Religion." *Ancient Mesoamerica* 16 (2005): 23–50.

———. "The Turquoise Hearth: Fire, Self-Sacrifice, and the Central Mexican Cult of War." In *Mesoamerica's Classic Heritage: From Teotihuacan to the Aztecs,* edited by Davíd Carrasco, Lindsay Jones, and Scott Sessions, 269–340. Boulder: University Press of Colorado, 2000.

———. "Through a Glass, Brightly: Recent Investigations Concerning Mirrors and Scrying in Ancient and Contemporary Mesoamerica." In *Manufactured Light: Mirrors in the Mesoamerican Realm,* edited by Emiliano Gallaga and Marc G. Blainey, 285–314. Boulder: University Press of Colorado, 2016.

Tedlock, Dennis, ed. and trans. *Popol Vuh.* New York: Simon and Schuster, 1985.

———. *Popol Vuh. The Maya Book of the Dawn of Life.* New York: Simon & Schuster, 1996.

Teeple, John E. "Maya Inscriptions, VI: The Lunar Calendar and Its Relation to Maya History." In *The Decipherment of Ancient Maya Writing*, edited by Stephen D. Houston, Oswaldo Chinchilla Mazariegos, and David Stuart, 207–9. Norman: University of Oklahoma Press, 2001.

Tezozómoc, Hernando Alvarado de. *Cronica Mexicana*. Mexico City: Editorial Porría, 1975.

Thompson, J. Eric S. *Maya Hieroglyphic Writing: An Introduction*. Norman: University of Oklahoma Press, 1960.

———. *Maya History and Religion*. Norman: University of Oklahoma Press, 1990.

Tokovinine, Alexandre. "The Western Sun: An Unusual Tzolk'in-Haab Correlation in Classic Maya Inscriptions." *The PARI Journal* 6, no. 2 (2010): 17–28.

Tucillo, Dylan, Jared Zeizel, and Thomas Peisel. *A Field Guide to Lucid Dreaming: Mastering the Art of Oneironautics*. New York: Workman, 2013.

Turner, Andrew. *Cultures at the Crossroads: Art, Religion, and Interregional Interaction in Central Mexico, AD 600–900*. PhD dissertation, Department of Anthropology, University of California at Riverside, March 2016.

Turner, Victor. *The Ritual Process: Structure and Anti-Structure*. Chicago: Aldine, 1969.

Umberger, Emily. *Aztec Sculptures, Hieroglyphs and History*. PhD dissertation, Graduate School of Arts and Sciences, Columbia University, 1981.

University of North Carolina at Charlotte. "Brief Meditative Exercise Helps Cognition." ScienceDaily (online), April 19, 2010.

Vail, Gabrielle. "Iconography and Metaphorical Expressions Pertaining to Eclipses: A Perspective from Postclassic and Colonial Maya Manuscripts." In Dowd and Milbrath: 163–96.

Vail, Gabrielle, and Anthony Aveni, eds. *The Madrid Codex*. Boulder: University Press of Colorado, 2004.

Vail, Gabrielle, and Victoria R. Bricker. "*Haab* Dates in the Madrid Codex." In Vail and Aveni: 171–214.

Walton, Alice G. "How to Kill a Thought (in a Good Way): More on Mindfulness." *Forbes* (website), June 20, 2012.

Watanabe, John M. "In the World of the Sun: A Cognitive Model of Mayan Cosmology." *Man* 18 (1983): 710–28.

Zavaleta, Antonio Noé. *Medicinal Plants of the Borderlands: A Bilingual Resource Guide*. Bloomington, Ind.: AuthorHouse, 2012.

Zavaleta, Antonio, and Alberto Salinas, Jr. *Curandero Conversations: El Niño Fidencio, Shamanism and Healing Traditions of the Borderlands.* Bloomington, Ind.: AuthorHouse, 2009.

Zender, Marc U. *A Study of Classic Maya Priesthood.* Thesis, Department of Archaeology, University of Calgary, July 2004.

# Index

Page numbers in *italics* indicate illustrations.
Numbers in *italics* preceded by *pl.* indicate color insert plate numbers.